S0-ATA-200

DATE DUE

MR 10 '86	_E3 '92	
MY 20 '86	_E29 '93	
JY 9 '86	_E05 '94	
OC 3 '88	_Y 17 '95	
MY 26 '87	_O28 '95	
JE 1 '87	OC 14 '96	
JY 6 '87	_E 5 '96	
JE 30 '88	JY 21 '97	
NO 16 '9_	DE 11 '97	
AP 2_	_E14 '99	
_E 30 '92	SE 22 '99	

Also by Jeanne Warren Lindsay:

Do I Have a Daddy?
A Story About a Single-Parent Child

Teens Parenting:
The Challenge of Babies and Toddlers

Pregnant Too Soon: Adoption Is an Option

TEENAGE MARRIAG

TEENAGE MARRIAGE: COPING WITH REALITY

By Jeanne Warren Lindsay

Morning Glory Press
Buena Park, California

Lindsay, Jeanne Warren
  Teenage Marriage.
  Bibliography: p.
  Includes index.
    1. Teen-age marriage. 2. Teen-age marriage--United
States. I. Title.
HQ799.2.M3L56 1984   306.8'1'088055   83-19638
ISBN 0-930934-12-1 (Hardcover)
ISBN 0-930934-11-3 (Trade)

MORNING GLORY PRESS
6595 San Haroldo Way   Buena Park, CA 90620
Telephone (714) 828-1998

To Bob
For Almost 33 Years
We Have Learned About Marriage Together.
I Love You Very!

Contents

FOREWORD   **11**

PREFACE   **13**

ACKNOWLEDGMENTS   **17**

INTRODUCTION   **20**

1. MARRIAGE—IS IT FOR YOU?   **23**
Facts about teenage marriage; Falling in love; Bonnie—married at 16; Importance of school; Should pregnancy mean marriage? Early marriage not recommended; Making marriage last; Trend toward "living together"; Is marriage forever?

2. I'LL FIND MY TRUE LOVE   **37**
Choosing a marriage partner; Agreement on expectations; Determination to succeed is important; Don't rush marriage; Similar interests help; Marriage won't solve family problems; Similar family backgrounds help; Possible problem areas

3. CHANGES...CHANGES... AND MORE CHANGES   **49**
Two kinds of changes; Teenagers change faster; Changes after marriage; Who picks up the socks? His family—her family: always different; Loneliness versus privacy; Change is inevitable

4. CREATIVE COMMUNICATION 57

Mixed messages cause problems; If he won't talk; Reasons for not talking; Plan time to talk; Handling arguments; Questions to ask yourself; Dealing with anger; "Wish list" approach; Different family scripts

5. SEX BEGINS IN THE KITCHEN 71

Effect of total relationship; How important is sex? Talk and compromise are essential; Conflict of expectations; Other problems with sex; Good relationship takes time; Effects of guilt feelings; Childbirth and sexual feelings; This, too, will pass; Sharing baby care helps; Sex is not a competition

6. ROLES—HIS JOB OR HERS? 83

Marriage roles are changing; Two-paycheck marriage preferred; Shared roles work; Two essentials: paycheck, housework; More women work today; Problem of housework; Psychologist suggests retraining; Sharing child care

7. THE BILLS AND BUDGET BLUES 97

Almost no income for some; Importance of job skills; Sharing money management; Who pays the bills? When a budget is necessary; Keep track of expenses; Cutting the costs of living; Making a budget; What about charge cards? Spending plan should suit you

8. MOVING-IN WITH IN-LAWS 113

It's hard to live with in-laws; Not enough privacy; Set up guidelines first; Who does the housework? Different backgrounds cause problems; Darla and Manuel's situation; Moving in with friends

9. CHILD-CREATED COMMOTION 127

Changes start with pregnancy; Marriage relationship is primary; Is education still important? Satisfying three people's needs; Father is full parent too; Helping dad feel capable; Good parenting takes learning; Grandparents get in the act; What about money? Another baby? When?

10. JEALOUSY—GREEN-EYED MONSTER   141
Marriage survey indicates jealousy; Reasons for jealousy; Lack of self-esteem; Jealousy related to possessiveness; If only one feels possessive; Coping with infidelity; If jealousy is severe; Solving the problem

11. PEOPLE ARE NOT FOR HITTING   153
Problem more severe for women; Battering compared to rape; Crisis center needed; Which men batter? Three-stage cycle described; Children affected if Dad hits Mother; Counseling may help; Characteristics of battered women; Why do they stay?

12. IF IT'S NOT FOREVER   165
It won't be easy; Immaturity can ruin relationship; Difference in values may destroy love; His reality is different; Counselor cautions against quick divorce; Professional counseling might help; If counseling fails; Grief of divorce; If a child is involved; Should you try again? The dilemma of step-children

13. DREAMS AND REALITY—MAKING IT WORK   177
She's pregnant—they marry; Living with parents; Victor walks out; She's pregnant again; Briann leaves town; Making a second start; Finally she can argue; Trust—hard to regain; She's less dependent; Explaining to Andrea

APPENDIX   187

I. Scorecard for Predicting Success of Teenage Marriage   188

II. Marriage Attitude Questionnaire   190

III. Annotated Bibliography   197

IV. Index   205

A Student Study Guide is available for *Teenage Marriage: Coping With Reality.* It is consumable and contains study questions and writing assignments for each chapter. Refer to last page of Appendix for ordering information or contact Morning Glory Press.

Foreword

In spite of high divorce rates and unenthusiastic scenarios, Americans obviously still believe in marriage. We continue to marry and, in many cases, remarry. Regardless of age and level of experience, most couples are still entering into marriage with the expectation that theirs will be satisfying, joyful, and committed. Couples still anticipate that their relationships will last. They are looking for partnerships that are mutually loving and supportive. In short, they are seeking the opportunity to experience a oneness with another human being.

As I work with today's young people, I find them dreaming of weddings, honeymoons, home lives, and families. In spite of all the warnings and negativity around us, I find these young people highly optimistic about their marital futures. Unfortunately, very few are prepared to meet the challenges faced by couples in today's society. Indeed, few have integrated the idea of potential pitfalls into their concepts of ideal marriage. Most lack the skills to work through the challenges of couplehood and parenthood. They need assistance in developing skills in communication and problem-solving. They need guidelines for formulating realistic expectations for their marriages.

Many fine books have already been written on this topic. However, in my experience, young people simply don't read them. These books are not geared to their needs. The pictures are of people of other generations. The people quoted are the ages of their parents. The language is difficult. So they leaf through these books and put them back on the shelf.

Jeanne Lindsay knows teenagers. She knows what appeals to them and what they'll read. I've watched hundreds of my counselees and students read her other books enthusiastically. I know young people will read this book.

Teenage Marriage: Coping with Reality is partly *by* teenagers and entirely *for* teenagers. This author does not guess about what teenagers want to know. She did vast research to prepare for this book. She asked thousands of teenagers about their beliefs and expectations. She interviewed many who have married. She shared her own thoughts and ideas. In the process, she does not separate herself from them by spouting platitudes.

Ms. Lindsay does not preach. She speaks from experience. This author loves teenagers and they love her. She is dedicated to sharing herself with them and to helping them share with each other. She listens, cares, laughs and cries. Her books reach the reader because she bridges gaps by touching their humanness with hers.

Catherine Monserrat
Counselor, New Futures School
Albuquerque, New Mexico
Co-Author: *Teenage Pregnancy: A New Beginning
Working with Childbearing Adolescents*

Preface

More than one million teenagers in the United States are married, according to *Teenage Pregnancy: The Problem That Hasn't Gone Away* (1981: The Alan Guttmacher Institute). These young marrieds comprise 8 percent of the female population aged 15-19 and 2 percent of the males in this age group.

Actually this is a sharp decrease since 1950 when 17.1 percent of the women aged 15-19 and 3.3 percent of the 15-19-year-old men were married, according to John R. Weeks, *Teenage Marriages: A Demographic Analysis* (1976: Greenwood Press). Today, however, many young people live together without benefit of a marriage ceremony. These young couples face many of the same adjustments experienced by young marrieds.

Our divorce statistics show that building a satisfying marriage relationship is difficult at any age. Developing and maintaining a good relationship is even harder for very young people. Adolescents experience tremendous changes during these years. Rapid change is part of the reason at least 60 percent of all teenage marriages fail within five years.

I have worked with school-age parents for eleven years. Some of these people are married and some are not. Many are coping amazingly well with early parenthood. Because our school offers childcare on campus, they are able to continue school after childbirth, gain job skills, and graduate from high school. According to research and my own observations, earning that high school diploma is an important factor in the development later of a lifestyle of choice.

Years ago, if a young single woman became pregnant, she was expected to marry the father of the baby. If they didn't marry, he was shirking his responsibilities and she was disgraced. "Shotgun" weddings are far less likely to occur today. Many young couples and their parents don't think getting married at an inopportune time makes an unplanned pregnancy "right."

About 365,440 teenagers who gave birth in 1978 were single when they conceived, according to the Alan Guttmacher Institute. More than 114,000 of these young women married before their babies were born. Other teenagers, of course, married before conception occurred.

Many young people marry for reasons other than or in addition to pregnancy. Like any other married couple, they hope to have a "happily ever after" marriage. Some of them will have satisfying, caring, loving, long-lasting relationships. Almost all want to develop a good relationship within their marriage.

Several factors make succeeding at marriage a real challenge for teenagers. Physical and emotional changes are not the only characteristics stacking the cards against teenage marriage. Lack of money is a big factor. Even if the husband is working, it's not likely he has a well-paying job. Many teenage brides are pregnant and unskilled; their chances of finding a good job are slim indeed.

The result is likely to be either dependency on welfare or on parents. Some of the young couples I interviewed make do on very little money. Sometimes there isn't enough cash to buy food and pay the rent.

Largely for financial reasons, teenage couples are likely to continue living with either his parents or hers after they marry and/or move in together. Almost always couples, whatever their age, find it difficult to live with parents-in-law. If either or both partners are still working through the adolescent stage of development with, typically, its attendant rebelliousness, even more problems are likely.

Most marriage books don't deal with the above problems. An author may include a chapter on financial planning, for example, but is more likely to discuss insurance and investments instead of ways of coping with almost no money. A discussion of in-law relationships usually assumes the young couple has separate living quarters. Jealousy and spousal abuse are seldom mentioned, yet many very young couples must deal with these problems.

Teenage Marriage: Coping With Reality deals with the special dilemmas faced by many young couples. As background, I completed a coast-to-coast survey of more than 3000 teenagers and their attitudes toward marriage. The questionnaire used for this survey, minus the biographical questions, is reproduced in the Appendix. Young couples are encouraged to answer the questions separately, then compare their answers as a means of learning more about each other.

Another book will be published which will detail the results of this survey. Of the 3,118 young people involved, 22.7 percent were male and 77.3 percent female. They represent all parts of the United States. The following charts provide more information on this group:

AGE:	14 or younger	15	16	17	18 or older
	8.6%	14.6%	24.9%	29.7%	22.2%

SCHOOL GRADE:	8 or lower	9-10	11	12	Not in school
	5.7%	35%	28.3%	27%	4%

PLACE OF RESIDENCE:	Inner City	Urban Area	Suburb	Town: 10,000 or less	Farm
	27.8%	21.7%	23.4%	16.8%	10.4%

ETHNIC GROUP:	White	Black	Latino/Hispanic	Asian	Native American
	58.8%	15.8%	23.4%	16.8%	10.4%

RELIGION:	Catholic	Protestant	"Born Again" Christians	Jewish	Other	None
	38%	13%	17%	1%	20%	11%

MARITAL STATUS:	Single	Engaged	Married	Separated	Divorced
	82.9%	10.7%	5.4%	.8%	.3%

While results of this survey are mentioned in nearly every chapter of *Teenage Marriage*, the book relies even more heavily on in-depth interviews with 55 young people. Included were 43 women, all former students of mine, and 12 men. Thirty-one were still teenagers at the time of the interview, and all the others were in their 20s. Represented were 28 married couples, four living-together couples, seven divorced women, and four single mothers. All of the married and divorced couples were married while one or both were teenagers. Length of their marriages at the time of the interview ranged from one to ten years. White, Hispanic, and Black couples were included.

These young people are the real experts, and they are quoted frequently. They share their hopes, their dreams, and their frustrations. They don't recommend very early marriage—many wish they had waited until they were older—but they do suggest ways of building a good relationship in spite of the difficulties they have faced.

Before making the decision to marry, they advocate learning as much as possible about each other. They often spoke of the lifetime commitment involved. Melinda and Greg were married nine years ago when she was 16 and he was 20. A few years ago they were almost divorced, but decided to continue trying to resolve their difficulties. Recently Melinda wrote:

> *I believe we will always be together because we have been through really rough times, nearly getting divorced, yet still loving one another. We both realize how much we want to be married to each other, and decided then that we'd give it all we had to make it work. And it's really been worth it!*
>
> *My advice to people who are thinking of getting married is to make a life-long commitment, try and learn all you can about the personality and values of the one you plan to marry, and share some of the same goals and ambitions for your life together. Then plan your life to give 110 percent of yourself to making it work.*
>
> *Believe the best in your partner and decide to love him/her even when you don't feel like it.*

Many of the other young people quoted in this book are coping quite well with their marriages, too. They have matured much faster than their ages indicate, and they offer suggestions for solving some of the problems which they have already faced in their relationships.

They aren't necessarily typical of married teenagers because only a few were divorced or contemplating divorce at the time of the interviews. I believed young people who were apparently building successful marriages could offer more helpful advice to others than would those whose marriages had ended. However, I felt comments from the interviewees who were already divorced added a necessary balance to this account of teenage marriage, and I appreciated their insight and sharing.

Although the divorce rate among married teenagers is very high, almost 90 percent of the 3,000 teenagers in the survey, most of them unmarried, expect their marriages to last a lifetime. *Teenage Marriage: Coping with Reality* offers suggestions which may help make this goal a reality for these young people.

Teenage Marriage is not meant to be an in-depth study of young marriage. Rather, it is designed to be read by the young people themselves, whether married, living together, or still single. Its purpose is to help these young people think seriously about the life-time commitment aspect of a good marriage and of ways to make this kind of marriage happen. Hopefully it will help these young people better understand and cope with some of the realities of their lives.

Acknowledgments

The teenagers I interviewed deserve the most credit for this book.
Without their help, *Teenage Marriage* would not have been written.
These young people shared their experiences in handling problems and in
developing caring, satisfying relationships with their partners. They hope
their insight will help others in their quest for a forever marriage.

Those interviewed who gave me permission to list their names
include Debbie and Mark Kruizenga, Gina and Wayne Pierce, Emelda
and Shannan Cottrell, Pauline and John Hill, Laura Gregor, Jeni
Vittori, Lupe and Bunji Cordi, Jana Williamson, Deborah and
Michael Spann, Veronica Nunez, Linda Lopez, Dianne Maher, Inez
Maldonado, Mary Garza, Pedro Sanchez, Shelly Ordiway, Eve
Wright, Darlene Comacho, Marilyn Markham, Terri Correa, Angel
Lucero, Connie Dominguez, Debbie Grinden, Linda Aguilar, Virginia
Cabrera, Margaret and Jerry Medina, Laureen Sauer, Erlinda Torres,
Lupe Rojas, Sylvia Pacheco, Christi Burstall, Susan Davis, Nora
Laredo, Joyce Costello, Yolanda Gonzales, Teri and Jim Unger, Rose
Mary Navarro, Vicki Kirby, Kara and Mario Zagone, Lisa Mojica,
Armando Gonzalez and Teri Tait.

More than 3,000 young people completed a lengthy questionnaire,
"Teenagers' Attitudes Toward Marriage." Each gave about an hour
of her/his time for this survey, and I appreciate them all. Those who
administered the questionnaire represented schools and other agencies
all over the United States. Their assistance was invaluable. Nick
Konnoff fed the 3,112 questionnaire answer sheets into the computer

at California State University, Long Beach. The result was a six-foot stack of computer paper analyses. I'm amazed. While these results are mentioned occasionally in this book, the results will be the basis of a book with a more analytical approach to teenage marriage.

Friends who gave information, advice and manuscript editing assistance include Sally McCullough, Jean Brunelli, Ellen Peach, Rita Blau, Bob and Jean Bayard, Marvin Greenbaum, Larry Treglia, Chuck Closson, Van Freemon, Julie Vetica, Eileen Cook, and Catherine Monserrat. Photographers were David Crawford, Bob Lindsay, and Vicki Golini. Pam Morford contributed the line drawings and Dave Hefner designed the cover.

My special love and appreciation go to Bob and Erin who were a tremendous help in producing *Teenage Marriage*...and to Steve who handled the typesetting and layout so capably.

Introduction

Coping with reality is what this book is all about. Whether you are single and alone, single but "with" somebody, or married, you're coping with your realities. That's what life is all about.

You'll find many quotes from married teenagers in these chapters. They talk about their realities as they struggle with lack of money, living with in-laws, extreme feelings of jealousy, and other problems. They also talk about the joys, the good things about their relationships.

Their comments have been edited slightly to mask their identities. Otherwise, all of the quotes in this book are "real," and are taken from conversations with young people who were married or living together while still teenagers.

Listening to young people talk about their realities as they struggle with relationships with partners may help you. If you are already married, you may understand some of their feelings very well. Joni was 15 when she and Jeff, 18, were married. Can you identify with the following comment she made about two years after their wedding?

> *When we got married both of us figured it was for keeps. It felt strange to move in together. We had to learn to grow toward each other, to adjust to each other's ways.*
>
> *We spent the first year learning what each was like. When you live with somebody, it's really different. But we still think our marriage is for keeps.*

If you aren't married, reading about the realities facing these young people may help you with your future plans. The ideas presented for creative communication, money management, and on other topics can be helpful whether or not you ever marry.

By the way, how to plan a wedding is not discussed in this book. For many couples, their wedding provides happy memories and holds great symbolic value. However, a lovely wedding doesn't guarantee a good marriage.

If you're planning your wedding now, whether a big and elaborate or small and intimate ceremony, enjoy. If you want advice, you'll find excellent books on the subject at your local library.

If you're married or you're planning to be married, you've undoubtedly been told over and over of the difficulties bound to occur in teenage marriage. You've probably heard that more than 60 percent fail within five years. But you know your marriage is/will be different.

Well, you can make yours different. You and your partner will need to work strenuously to keep your relationship going. Perhaps you already have several strikes against you. Maybe you have no money, you're living with his parents, and you have a baby you hadn't planned to have. It all sounds pretty difficult. But other couples in your situation have developed life-long satisfying and caring relationships. The majority of teenage marriages fail, but you don't need to be part of that majority. Early marriage is hard on the couples involved, but beautiful relationships can develop.

All marriages have problems as well as joys. If a couple insists they have no problems, their marriage is likely to be in trouble. They aren't facing reality. Problem-solving is an important part of any successful marriage. Ways to solve some of the inevitable problems will be discussed in this book.

Sometimes a problem becomes easier to deal with if you know you aren't the only one with such a problem. Hearing someone else talk about her feelings of jealousy, for example, may help you look more realistically at your own situation.

However, you'll probably learn more by listening to young people explain why they think their marriages are "beating the odds." While I interviewed a few divorced people, I spent more time with teenagers whose marriages appear to be working. They often shared possible reasons for their success.

If it's a forever marriage you and your partner want, then you need to start today—or continue—working on that journey to forever... together.

Chapter 1

> *You have to feel it's right. It can't be because you're pregnant or because you're by yourself or you want to get out of the house. You have to have mutual love, some of the same likes, some of the same goals. You can't have a marriage when one person wants to go his way and the other wants to go another way.*

(Bonnie, married at 16 to Jess, 23)

Marriage...
Is It For You?

When "should" a young couple get married? Is there a "right" age? Is there a sure way to measure your readiness and your partner's readiness for marriage?

Of course, there is no magic ruler which will measure a specific couple's chance of being happy and satisfied with each other for the rest of their lives. Each couple must decide whether *they* are ready to commit themselves to each other. If you aren't already married, this book may help you decide if, when, and whom you want to marry.

Facts About Teenage Marriage

If you aren't yet 18, the law may influence your decision about marriage. In California, if either partner is under 18, the couple may be married only if they have parental consent for the person(s) under 18, permission of the Superior Court, and proof of premarital counseling for both. Other states have different requirements. Call the office of your County Clerk for information or see your pastor, priest or rabbi.

As a group, couples in their teens have less chance of having a long-term marriage than do older couples. At least 60 percent of those who marry before they are 20 will be divorced within five years.

More than 3,000 teenagers from different parts of the United States completed a long questionnaire in which they shared their attitudes about marriage. Results of this survey will be mentioned throughout this book.

At least 85 percent of these young people thought both men and women should wait until age 20 or older to get married. More than one-fifth thought women should be at least 25. Even more, about one-third, said men should be 25 years old or older when they marry. Some individuals, of course, do not plan ever to be married.

In spite of these statistics, many teenagers do marry, and some of these marriages are long-lasting. As one happily-married young husband put it, "It feels good to be beating the odds—to know we're making it even though we were only 18 when we married."

Falling in Love

Have you "fallen in love"? Dr. Charles Closson, marriage and family counselor in Anaheim, California, claims that falling in love has nothing to do with "real" love. It's a separate thing which he calls a mating ritual. "It's a kind of blindness that says, 'I have to be with this person,' and it's always a sexual thing," he commented.

"Real love is trust, respect and caring," he continued. "When you fall in love, the tingle eventually fades. But if, in addition to falling in love, you trust, respect and care for the other person, you'll continue to love. Friendship ought always to precede marriage, and friendship is trust, respect and caring."

"Growing into love" rather than "falling in love" will provide a good foundation for a happy, satisfying marriage.

The young couples in this chapter talk about the difficulties of early marriage, but most of them are still together. Looking at some of the reasons a marriage is lasting may be more helpful than reading only about the problems involved in very early marriage.

Bonnie—Married at 16

Jess and Bonnie's marriage seemed doomed. They were married when she was 16 and he was 23. He had been married before. She was still in high school. Their friends were shocked.

Five years and two children later, they are together and appear happy with their relationship. I asked Bonnie for advice for other 16-year-olds.

I've talked to a lot of people about that. It's right for some people and not for others. In my case, it was something that personally I had to do, that I felt was right.

I think that's the main thing you have to do. It can't be because you're pregnant or because you're by yourself or want to get out of the house. You have to have mutual love, some of the same likes, some of the same goals. You can't have a marriage when one person wants to go this way and the other wants another way. You have to talk it over.

Even before I met Jess, I always thought about getting married, having children, living happily ever after. Then after I met him, it all just happened.

But it didn't "just happen." Bonnie and Jess have worked hard to keep their marriage together. In their favor was the fact that Bonnie wasn't pregnant when they got married. A heavy strain is placed on teenagers who are adjusting to parenthood at the same time they're learning to live with each other.

Bonnie mentioned that loneliness or wanting to "get out of the house" are *not* good reasons to get married. Marriage is seldom an escape from problems. The problems may change, but they won't disappear.

Often if the wife is very young when she marries a man a few years older, she plays a very dependent role. At first, both she and her husband think he should be in charge. As she matures, however, she may tire of this little-girl role. Sometimes the man can't handle it when his formerly dependent wife develops a mind of her own.

Somehow, in spite of their age difference, Bonnie and Jess have developed a style in their marriage which suits them both. From the beginning Bonnie and Jess both assumed they were partners. Both wanted an equal marriage.

Importance of School

It was important to both that Bonnie finish high school. She became pregnant a few months after their wedding. They moved three times during her pregnancy. She found a special class for pregnant teenagers in each of the three communities. Her senior year was not like that of most high school students, but she did graduate two months after Jennie was born. Jess held Jennie as he cheered his beaming wife as she walked down the aisle in her light blue cap and gown.

We've had problems, lots of them, but the main thing is to talk it over and work it out. Even if you can't work it out, at least talk about it and try to solve it. So many people think it's going to work out by itself. But it just doesn't happen that way.

I had Jennie 14 months after we were married, Susie two years later. I love my kids and I would probably do the same thing if I could start over. But it's real hard—I don't say it's easy—and sometimes I wish it hadn't happened. Our marriage is by no means perfect—I never pretended it was—but all in all, I'm glad. I'm happy with Jess.

Many married teenagers drop out of school. For many years, teenagers who were either pregnant or married (or both) were expected to leave school. They weren't allowed to stay. That has changed. It's now against the law for a school to drop a student because of pregnancy, marriage, or parenthood. Many, many young people still drop out of school, however, when they get married or when they become pregnant.

Most of us know young women who quit school because of pregnancy. In fact, studies show more girls drop out of school because of pregnancy than for any other reason. She is even more likely to drop out of school if she's married than if she's single and pregnant.

Young couples and young single mothers and fathers who manage to stay in school have a *much* better chance of getting and keeping good jobs after they graduate. According to research, they are less likely to have a second baby before they're ready for him/her. Both factors help prevent the lifetime of poverty faced by so many who have their first child before they finish school.

Bonnie's last year in school was very hard for her. She would rather have been home, but she decided—and Jess agreed—that it was worth the sacrifice. Their marriage is undoubtedly stronger because of that decision.

Should Pregnancy Mean Marriage?

Most people in our culture think that ideally a couple is married before pregnancy begins. But what if she gets pregnant before they're married? In the past, this usually meant a "shotgun" wedding. Parents often pushed for a quick wedding "to make it right." But a quick wedding doesn't necessarily make it right if you consider marriage a life-long commitment. Rosemarie was in eleventh grade,

Steve in tenth, when she discovered she was pregnant. She learned too late
that not thinking about "whether it would last forever" was a mistake:

> *On a Monday we told my parents I was pregnant. On Saturday
> we found ourselves in Las Vegas getting married!*
>
> *I really didn't think about whether it would last forever. I
> thought it was a way to correct my problem. I think it was
> something I didn't honestly want, but my mother insisted. I don't
> even remember what happened that week. I think if I had had a
> couple more weeks to think about it, I probably wouldn't have
> done it.*
>
> *Our marriage lasted less than three years. Our son is five now.
> Because of visitation rights I'll have Steve around for the next 13
> years whether I want to or not. And we don't get along.*
>
> *I finished high school, but Steve dropped out to work full-time.
> He still to this day blames me for him never finishing school. He
> says, "You messed me up so I could never graduate."*

Being blamed for your spouse never finishing high school would be
rough. "If we hadn't married I would have..." is often a painful
thought. Before rushing into early marriage, both partners need to feel
sure neither will put that guilt trip on the other at some time in
the future.

Eighteen months after her divorce, Rosemarie married Bob. She compared her readiness for marriage in each case:

> I wasn't ready for marriage the first time. I wasn't mature enough to handle all the responsibilities that were being put on me. I wasn't ready to make a home life yet. Even though I had been dating for a year before we were married, I still wanted to date, and I felt like I was missing out.
>
> But I wanted to get married this time. I didn't have to. Between the time I got divorced and started seeing Bob, I had time to be on my own. That was when I decided marriage was what I wanted instead of being forced into it. That time between marriages helped a lot.
>
> Although Steve and I had known each other more than a year, we never really talked about ourselves. We just went out. Bob and I knew more about each other before we got married than I ever knew about my first husband. We knew our goals, what we wanted to do.

Only one in eight of the teenagers in the survey said a pregnant high school-age couple "absolutely" should get married. An additional one-fourth of the girls and one-third of the boys thought this couple probably should marry. The rest felt it was important to base a marriage on choice rather than force. Melodie, pregnant at 16, shared her opinion:

> I don't think anyone should rush into marriage even if she's pregnant. That's a big mistake people make. Brett's mom wanted us to go to Reno for a $25 wedding just because of what other people would think. But I don't believe in worrying about what other people think.
>
> If you're getting married for any reason other than love and companionship, how is it going to work? I remember Sally saying she didn't want to embarrass her father by walking down the aisle pregnant. So she hurried up and got married before she showed. That's ridiculous—getting married because of other people. Sally is already divorced.
>
> My father sat us down and said, "It would be nice if you guys got married." But he didn't push us. We waited until Donna was nine months old, when we knew we were ready. I had a chance to have a wedding dress, to make it something special. I feel real good about our marriage. (Melodie, married at 17 to Brett, 19)

Early Marriage Not Recommended

When asked why she, at 17, and Rick, 18, got married while she was in high school, Tammy replied:

> *Because we were pregnant plus we were in love. We wanted to get married before Lisa was born so we could be together and share all the experiences.*
>
> *But I hope Lisa waits longer. I'll advise her not to go too steady with a guy right away. I'll tell her to go out and date a lot of different guys and not to think the first one is the right one. There are a lot of different guys out there, and you have got to make sure it's the right one before you get too serious. It's always hard to break up a serious relationship.*
>
> *If I hadn't gotten pregnant, I probably wouldn't be married now. I've been out of school almost a year, and I think I'd be ready perhaps next year when I'll be 19 or 20.*
>
> *I don't think Rick would be doing what he's doing now if we hadn't gotten married. He had to work full-time for us to live. He was forced to choose a career right away. He's trying to work at it plus go to school at night and learn about it there. I think if things had been different he would have taken his time and gone into something else.*

Elaine, married five years ago at 17 to Lloyd, 19, was even more outspoken with her advice.

> *Advice on early marriage? I'd tell her not to do it. Finish school for heaven's sake, go to college, get a career, then fall in love and get married after you find what you want to do with your life. I hope my daughter doesn't get pregnant or married that young. Getting pregnant is bad enough but marriage really ties me down.*
>
> *I'm still so young and there is so much I want to do—but I have the girls. I'm not complaining—I wouldn't give them up for the world. But there are times when I wish I were 16 again and could go to maybe 27 before I have kids.*
>
> *I want to be an R.N. I've started school twice and quit both times. Lloyd doesn't want to watch the kids, so I've had to drop out.*
>
> *I think early marriage is foolish for a young man too. Lloyd feels the same way. We both wish we could have waited until we were 27 or 28. When we first met, I got pregnant right away. He wanted the*

baby and he wanted me—he never turned his back on us. But it was too early, we were too young. It breaks my heart to see 13- and 14-year-old girls pregnant. But you can't tell teenagers anything. Nobody could tell me anything.

Making Marriage Last

All of the young people quoted above except Rosemarie are still married. If, as they suggest, married life is so hard for very young people, why haven't their marriages failed?

The main reason, undoubtedly, is the fact that each has worked hard at staying together. They didn't marry because they "had to." They chose to marry while they were quite young, even though they knew there would be struggles ahead.

While they spoke of money problems, most of these young couples did not have to rely either on parents or on welfare for financial support. Being able to support oneself is generally a sign of maturity.

Most people agree that maturity is one of the basic ingredients needed for building a long-lasting, satisfying marriage.

These young people often spoke of the importance of talking through their problems, the need for good communication. Joni and Jeff are good examples. She was a tenth grader and 15 when she became pregnant. Jeff, 18, had graduated a few months earlier. He had a fairly good job. Joni talked about the changes in their lives, the decisions they had to make:

> *We have both matured a lot. We had to. One day I found out I was pregnant, and that night I grew up so fast! Another life was coming into both of ours, and we had to adjust to it.*
>
> *We had talked about marriage, but we had broken up before I knew I was pregnant. Finally one night Jeff took me out to dinner and we talked. That's when I told him I suspected I was pregnant.*
>
> *He took me to have the test done the next day and he paid for it. But we didn't get back together for about two months although we often talked. It was hard—I needed somebody then. Finally one day he told me, "Joni, I love you." I knew I loved him too. That night at his house he asked me, "Will you marry me?" I said "Yes." Our mothers were real happy but I think both dads had their doubts.*

Angela was born two months after they were married. Two years later Joni graduated from high school, to her parents' amazement and to her delight. Their marriage has had its ups and downs including a brief separation last year, but they feel quite positive about their relationship.

In a conversation about 15 months after their wedding, both offered some advice for other young people and for their daughter:

> Joni: *Advice? Both of us would suggest they wait, learn to know each other more. I wouldn't want Angela to be married at 15. I don't mean to be mean, but I would try to talk her out of it. I want her to get her education, to know something about life before she even thinks of marriage. That's what I wanted, and I'm sure Jeff did too. It's hard even though things are going great right now. It's hard.*
>
> Jeff: *Yes, you need to live your life when you're young. There's always time for marriage later.*
>
> Joni: *It's not easy at all. There's so much that we miss out on. Jeff had his early life, but I really didn't.*
>
> Jeff: *She's right. I got to do things on my own when I was a kid. But she didn't. She was married at 15. But it's getting better.*

A few months after the above conversation, Joni took Angela back to her parents' home to live for awhile. She had a brief fling at the freedom she thought she had been missing, but that didn't satisfy her either. At this time she and Jeff are back together again.

Trend Toward "Living Together"

The percentage of young women marrying while still teenagers has been decreasing in the United States. Now only about 8 percent marry before reaching age 20. Twenty-five years ago about twice that many were married while in their teens.

Part of this change is because of the current trend for more couples to live together before they get married. In this book, most of the comments concerning relationships can be applied to living-together couples as well as to legally-married partners.

For some people, living together before marriage is acceptable. For others, it's not. More than half the boys but only 40 percent of the girls in the marriage survey said it was OK. An additional one-fourth said it was all right *if* they plan to marry later. More than 17 percent of the girls and 12 percent of the boys think it's wrong to do so. The rest responded, "It's OK but I wouldn't do it."

Rosemarie, whose first and very early marriage ended in divorce, and who is now happily married to Bob, gave her viewpoint on the living together issue:

> *Live together before marriage? I'm not a good person to ask because I'm totally against it. I think it's wrong for me, but I don't put other people down for doing it. Granted you may become more at ease with each other living together—but I think you can find out quite a lot about one another without living together.*
>
> *I think I like feeling secure. I don't want to get that involved, then have him say, "Well, I don't want to live here anymore." Both of my older brothers lived with their wives before they got married. I don't think it hurt their relationship, but I don't really think it helped either.*

Darla, who lived with Manuel for awhile when she was 16 and he was 20, has a different viewpoint:

> *To me it seems like living together and being married are two different things. It's doing the same things, but being married ties*

*you down more. You know he'll be coming home and you have
to do everything he wants. I would rather live together first to see
how it is.*

Annie, 15, and Jose, 17, lived together for several months after
their baby was born. Then they decided to get married. She said:

> *There wasn't really a difference between living together and being
> married. We got along a little better after our wedding. The
> housework was the same, but somehow our relationship was better.*
> *I guess part of it was I felt more committed to him. I wanted
> to get married. For a long time most of our fights were over the
> fact that we weren't married. Somehow getting married showed
> me how much he loved me, that he wanted to make a commit-
> ment. Once we got married I started feeling better about him and
> I guess he started feeling better about me too.*

For some people, living together may help prepare them for
marriage. Others feel they can learn enough about each other through
dating with no need or desire for a living-together period. For others,
the choice doesn't exist—they simply feel living together without
marriage is wrong.

> *We weren't living together before we got married. I have
> always been brought up that it's not right, that you should be
> married. That's one of the things to look forward to when you
> get married. You live together and you sleep together and you're
> with each other all the time. I would never have lived with him if
> we hadn't gotten married.* (Tammy, married at 17 to Rick, 18)

Moving in together would probably be a bad decision if either of
you thinks it isn't right to do so. One of you may want to get married
while the other thinks simply living together would be better. If this is
so, you disagree on a very basic issue, and you would be wise to
postpone both marriage and living-together for awhile.

Is Marriage Forever?

About half of today's marriages end in divorce. But this is *not* what
teenagers want, according to the survey. Two-thirds said "Absolutely"
when asked if marriage was "Forever," and another 21 percent said
"Probably," a total of almost nine in ten.

Almost 200 married and/or living-together teenagers answered the open-ended question, "Do you think your partnership will last 'forever'? Please comment." Only 40 percent of those young people said "Yes," compared to almost 90 percent of the total sample who *want* marriage to be forever. Seventeen had already split up, although four hoped they would get back together. One person wrote, *"Now* is wonderful—that's all that matters."

Darci, married at 18, cautions:

> *If you really aren't sure, give yourself time. Make sure everything is planned. Don't rush into anything you may be sorry for.*

Chapter 2

> We mostly like to do the same
> things. We walk along the beach
> and go out on the pier at night. We
> both love to fish and we go to
> concerts together.
>   Going out together, learning and
> experiencing things together is good
> for a marriage. To experience first-
> time things with someone you love
> is neat.

(Pati, married at 17 to Mike, 18)

I'll Find
My True Love

> *We try to do things together. I don't mean to leave Gloria out*
> *of anything I do. At the same time we try to give each other*
> *freedom so it's a pretty good balance.*
>
> *I have a little less time alone but I've gotten used to it. I think*
> *when you're married you should try to share things.* (Derek,
> married at 18 to Gloria, 18)

If you expect to be married sometime in the future, what type of
person do you want to marry? If you're already married, what was
there about your mate that made you decide to choose him/her as
your spouse?

The ideal person for you might be quite different from the person
considered ideal by your best friend. But you'd probably agree that
you want to love and be loved. That's pretty basic. You also want
someone you can trust, respect, and care for and who will trust,
respect, and care for you. These factors are a basic part of love, as
described by Dr. Charles Closson in the last chapter.

After these basic characteristics you could get more specific. If you
and your partner share some of the same interests, that's a plus. If
you can talk and be open with each other, that's a plus. If you argue,
fight, disagree on almost everything, that's a minus—even if you're
madly in love!

Choosing a Marriage Partner

Luckily, a happy marriage doesn't depend on a special type of
person. Outgoing fun-loving people always on the go can be happily
married. So can people who want to sit home most of the time, people
who prefer an evening with a good book instead of in the company of
a television set. The secret is for two partners to have interests which,
if not the same, at least complement each other.

Opposites may attract, but if they have nothing in common, the
attraction may not last long. It's possible for a quiet person to enjoy
being with someone who talks to everybody and who is always the life
of the party. Over the years this might not be a happy situation.

Annalee, married at 17 to Curt, 20, doesn't think their marriage will
last much longer. She's finding that she and Curt have much less in
common than she had realized when they married:

> *I guess one of our biggest problems is that he likes to stay*
> *home so much. He doesn't want to take me anywhere.*

On Sunday he'll just lay there and watch TV. I'll say, "Let's take the baby to church," but he won't. I'll fix him a big breakfast, and then he'll lie there and start napping. I always want to go someplace but he won't leave.

Before you marry, learn as much as you possibly can about your partner. Finding out after marriage that you don't like to do the same things could be a disaster.

Notice how your partner interacts with your friends and your family. Sometimes a young couple gets along wonderfully when they're alone. When they're with friends or family, however, one or both may find the other "acts different."

If you feel uncomfortable when you and your partner are with other people, try to figure out reasons for your feelings. Hopefully, you will work it out *before* you marry. Forever is a long time to be uncomfortable when you and your spouse are with other people.

Three things are especially important in a couple learning to adjust to each other, according to Dr. Tom McGinnis, author of *Your First Year of Marriage* (1977: Wilshire Book Company, p. 9). The first is personality fit. Does your partner have ways of feeling and acting, of *being*, that you do or would find comfortable to live with? Do your ways of acting and being please your partner?

If you're "in love," you're likely to say "Yes" to these questions. Common sense tells us we usually like being with the person we love.

But think ahead to how you may feel about your partner several years from now. Will that charming fun-loving relaxed attitude she has still be as charming if she's so relaxed she doesn't find and keep a good job—yet you need two paychecks to survive? Will his admirable habit of always looking and dressing beautifully still be as admirable if there isn't enough money to pay for the clothes he buys?

Agreement on Expectations

This leads into Dr. McGinnis' second point which he titles "Agreement on Expectations." Does each of you have about the same ideas as to how a husband and wife should act? This includes issues such as who does what around the house, parenting expectations, and money management goals. Do you agree on what you expect of each other?

We talked a lot before we got married—what we wanted in life, how we wanted children, how we wanted to raise them, about

schooling. We felt pretty much the same about almost everything.
You have to talk about your problems and about everything
else. Talk about what you want, what colors you like, everything.
(Bonnie, married at 16 to Jess, 23)

You need to talk about various kinds of expectations. First, do you have similar values? Do you agree on the importance (or unimportance) of education? Is one of you more concerned about thinking in the future while the other tends to be present-oriented? For example, you might want to plan and sacrifice now so you can buy that home of your dreams. Your partner may put higher priority on enjoying life today.

The Day the Senior Class Got Married, a novel by Gloria Miklowitz (1983: Delacourte) is the story of a young couple, both seniors in high school, who are planning to be married. As the months pass, however, Lori realizes she is a future-oriented person while her boyfriend lives for the present. The book provides a good and highly interesting description of some of the problems which can occur in such a situation.

Do you agree on whether or not you want to have children? Many couples today are delaying pregnancy until each has a chance to get a strong career going. Other couples decide never to have children. Others want several children as quickly as possible. A satisfying life is possible with or without children. The problem starts when one of you wants a baby and the other one doesn't. Or perhaps you have one child, and you would like another but your partner says one is enough:

Dale doesn't want anymore and that's kind of bad. When I see
a little baby I want one so bad. But Dale says, "No, we're
young, we have a whole life ahead of us." And we really didn't
have much time to do things together before Chrissie was born.
He wants her to grow up so we can spend more time by our-
selves. (Arlene, married at 18 to Dale, 18)

If you want children, have you discussed childcare? Not only how the work and joys will be divided, but *how* you want to raise your kids. If one of you "knows" kids have to be spanked in order to become civilized while the other one says firmly, "People are not for hitting," how will you cope?

Have you discussed how you feel about the importance of work and career versus time spent with your family? If one of you is ambitious and expects to work very hard to get ahead while the other thinks it's more important to spend time at home, you'll have trouble.

Little things may wreck more marriages than the big ones. Have you talked about who does the housework, the cooking, the laundry? (Come to think about it, these aren't "little" things.) Who will mow the lawn? Fix the car?

The list could go on endlessly and you'll never find two people who agree perfectly on everything (unless one is a terrible liar.) But at least know where you differ before you commit yourself to a marriage which, hopefully, will continue throughout your life.

Determination to Succeed Is Important

The third thing stressed by Dr. McGinnis is that you both be determined to succeed in your marriage. Will both of you work through disappointments and disagreements to make your marriage a deeply satisfying experience for both of you? If so, you'll be closer to achieving a "forever" marriage.

Jess said we were going to make this marriage work whether we wanted to or not! Sometimes we felt like saying, "Let's just give it up." Those were the times we'd sit down and talk and try to figure out what was going wrong. We hold each other. If you want to cry, you cry on the other person's shoulder. That has happened a lot with us. (Bonnie)

I'm stubborn, and I made up my mind our marriage would work. It's been hard. Of course we've argued, but we end up talking things out. Walt tries to understand me. He's a good listener. (Marcella, married eight years ago at 15 to Walt, 19)

Don't Rush Marriage

Marrying someone soon after you meet him/her is risky. If you haven't had time to know each other well, you won't know whether your personalities "fit." It will be difficult for either of you to know what to expect of the other in your relationship. And in a brief whirl-wind courtship it is impossible really to know how much each is willing to sacrifice in order for the marriage to succeed.

Once you and your partner decide to get married, it's wise to wait awhile longer. Some experts recommend an engagement period of six months to a year. Instead of "falling into love," you have a chance to "grow into love."

We were boyfriend/girlfriend four years before we got married and I feel we knew each other very well. That ironed out a lot of potential difficulties. We were lucky in that, I think. We knew each other very well before we got pregnant.

Of course there were still surprises. You don't find out a lot of things about a person until you live with her. (Derek)

Similar Interests Help

More than 90 percent of the boys and even more of the girls in the marriage attitudes survey thought it was important for a couple to share common interests. Sharing interests is a good foundation for marriage. If you and your partner don't like to do some of the same things, you'll find it's hard to maintain a close relationship.

Are you a homebody? Or do you prefer to spend most of your time out doing things with your friends? Are you and your partner mostly in agreement on this issue?

> *We're real homebodies. I think a lot of the problem with couples we know who have split is that they were always out there doing things, spending money they didn't have. I think we're each other's best friend—and that's what you need to do in a marriage.* (Kent, married at 19 to Amy, 19)

Yvette and Vince were married when she was 17 and he was 19. One common interest is that they share the same career dream:

> *He wants to be a mechanic and I'd like to be the same thing. We're going to a bodyshop class together this fall. Right now he's working for someone else and doing bodyshop work here at home. He doesn't have all the tools but he's getting them. I already help him a lot.*
>
> *He says he doesn't want to work for someone else. Both of us will work here. I like to get dirty and little Vince is here with us getting dirty too. We can make quite a lot of money because we'll have our own business.*

Some couples like to spend most of their time together. Others would find it hard to work closely all day, every day with their spouses. Neither way is right or wrong. The important thing is for both partners to agree on this issue. If they do, either way of thinking and acting can be the basis for a satisfying marriage.

Whether or not you and your spouse want to work together, it's important that each of you has interests of your own. Relying entirely on another person for everything is not wise. If you have some separate activities, you'll find you have more to talk about when you are together.

Donita and Ray were married seven years ago when she was 17, a senior in high school, and he was 18. They have worked out a satisfying lifestyle although they aren't involved in a lot of activities together:

> *We haven't had too many interests in common. He goes fishing and golfing and I don't. But it doesn't bother me because I like to stay home and do things I like to do. I'm sure he likes to be with his brothers.*
>
> *We see each other all day—he works nights—and I think it's*

*good to get away from each other occasionally. We sometimes go
out to eat and to the show, but not much else together.*

Sometimes it's hard to understand if your spouse has interests which
don't include you. Gloria was unhappy for awhile because of Derek's
music. She's found an interesting solution:

*Derek likes to spend a lot of time by himself and I didn't know
that. He's really into his music and that was a problem. He'd be
gone all day and I'd expect him to spend time with me when he
came home. Instead, he comes in, picks up his guitar, and is
completely oblivious of me.*

*I didn't like that but I'm learning. I used to always want to
sing. I guess I was jealous of him because he's in a band. But
now I've gotten into a singing group with my brother. Now I'm
easing up with Derek because I know more about where he's
coming from. I know how he feels.*

Marriage Won't Solve Family Problems

Some young people get married to escape a bad family situation:

*When I was with my family I had a lot of trouble. I was so
confused when I got married that I don't even understand why
it's working. I think my parents should have given me a chance to
grow up. But they didn't allow me to have a boyfriend or to go
out. When I married Walt, he was somebody to save me. He felt
the same way because he had some depressing things going on
with his mother. We needed each other.*

*If my parents had given me a chance, I think I wouldn't have
gotten married at 16. But I wanted to show them. When Walt
came around, I felt he was there to hold me and to take care of
me. When we became lovers I felt he was the whole world and it
didn't matter what my parents did. They were driving me closer
to him.* (Marcella)

If there are too many rules at home, marriage can look like a lot of
freedom. "If I get married, no one can tell me what to do," they say.
But it doesn't often work this way according to Rita Blau, clinical
psychologist at the Intercommunity Child Guidance Center, Whittier,
California.

"A lot of young people want to escape, get out of the house. They think getting married and/or having a baby will do this. But they don't have money, and they're still facing the same family problems they had before," she said.

"Often the problem gets bigger," she continued. "If you're a teenager living with your parents, you're likely to have some problems. That's part of being an adolescent. But if you have a spouse and/or a baby, you'll find it's even harder to cope." Marriage seldom solves problems with one's parents.

What about your partner's parents? Two important questions to ask yourself are: "Do I like my partner's parents?" and "Does s/he like mine?" You aren't marrying your in-laws, but they're an important part of your spouse's life. Since your spouse is/will be such an important part of your life, your relationship with your in-laws can strongly affect your marriage. If you can start your life together with the approval of all your parents, your marriage will have a better chance of succeeding.

If you don't like your partner's parents and/or think they don't like you, what can you do to improve the situation? If you're living with them, it's even more important that you get along well. Talking through your concerns with them might be a good start.

If you don't live with them, do you see them very often? Do you try to be friendly? Young people sometimes say to me, "I don't like his family so I don't talk to them. I just stay out of their way." This is not a good way to improve the situation. If you think his/her family seems unfriendly, you need to try even harder to create a good relationship with them.

Similar Family Backgrounds Help

Do you and your partner belong to the same ethnic group? Are your family backgrounds similar? Is your religious faith similar to your partner's?

Some happily-married couples grew up in very different family situations. However, couples with similar backgrounds tend to have fewer problems over the years.

If you decide to marry someone from a different ethnic group and/or religion, your parents are likely to disapprove. You and your partner will need to compromise on a number of issues. But it can work. Donita and Ray, married seven years, belong to two very different churches. They discussed their solution:

Donita: *We're very different on this, and you'd think we'd clash a lot. I think I'm a pretty firm church member—at least I try to be. I go to church all the time. But he doesn't go very often, just Christmas and Easter. But he's real open-minded. So many parents want their kids to marry someone in the same religion—I know my parents would have preferred that.*

Ray: *I wish she belonged to my church because she'd make me go. But I don't want to go to her church, so I don't go at all.*

Donita: *I won't push him. I invite him occasionally, but I don't bug him. I feel that if this is the religion for him, God will do it, not me. I do take the kids to my church.*

Ray: *At least they're going. That's what matters.*

Agreeing on religion means one less problem in a marriage. But if two people belong to different churches, they can each continue in his/her own. If they have children, they will need to work out an agreement on their religious experiences. A compromise may be especially hard to work out if both partners feel very strongly about their own faith. Talk it through before you get married.

Possible Problem Areas

A young person "surviving" on a skimpy allowance from parents might think marriage would mean more money. If that person's future spouse is earning a regular paycheck, it's probably quite a lot more than the allowance from Mother and Dad.

However, most of the young people I interviewed expressed shock and concern about their financial situation. They hadn't expected so many bills. If they made the rent payment they couldn't afford the refrigerator they needed. Each time they saved a little money, it had to be spent for unexpected doctor bills or other emergencies. See Chapter 8 for their comments.

Do you and your partner argue a lot? If your answer is "No, never," you're likely to have as many problems as the couple who argues too much. Never arguing means one of you is in charge and the other is going along with whatever the other person suggests. That's not good for either one of you.

On the other hand, if you and your partner argue constantly, how do you feel about continuing your relationship? A lifetime of fighting doesn't sound like much fun. Chapter 4, which discusses communication, might help in either case.

Does either of you think the other one has a drug or alcohol problem? The effects of overuse of drugs and/or alcohol have ruined many marriages. Your wedding won't change the situation.

What about jealousy? Trust is an important factor in a good marriage. If your partner is upset if you look at or talk to another person of the opposite sex, trust appears to be lacking. See Chapter 10 for a discussion of jealousy.

Is either your father or your partner's father into hitting his wife? An alarmingly high percentage of men whose fathers were violent are violent themselves. Women who grew up seeing their mothers beaten tend to accept that kind of life for themselves. See Chapter 11 for more information about this problem.

One of the most positive aspects of a good marriage is a couple who feel good about themselves. The person who doesn't think highly of her/himself generally has a harder time forming a close relationship with someone else. High self-esteem on the part of both partners provides a wonderful foundation for a marriage.

Finally, another very important question: Does either you or your partner (or both) have a job which provides enough money to meet your expenses? Two *cannot* live as cheaply as one!

If you're both in high school, you may need help from your parents. If you have a child, you may qualify for AFDC (Aid for Families with Dependent Children) while you finish school.

If you need financial help to finish high school, you'll be ahead if you accept that help. Most people don't like to accept welfare. Even if you qualify for this kind of aid, you won't get enough to live as you'd like to live. But if that's what it takes for you to get an education so you can be independent later on, the sacrifice will be worthwhile.

On page 188 you'll find a "Scorecard for Predicting Success of Teenage Marriage." If you're thinking of getting married, sit down with your partner and "test" your chances of having a successful marriage. If your score is low, you might be wise to wait awhile before you marry.

But you may already be married and you find your score is not as high as you'd like. That's a sign that you and your partner need to work especially hard at making your relationship succeed. Good luck!

Forever is a long time. You can have some control over your forever by choosing carefully the person you marry.

Chapter 3

*Before you're married you love
each other as two complete individuals. But after you're married you
change a lot and you have to love
the person he becomes. When you
start being together 24 hours a day,
you learn a lot about each other's
faults, and they're completely
different. When you aren't living
together you can hide them...you can
seem to be something you aren't. But
you really get to know somebody
after you get married.*

(Lena, married at 16 to Tom, 18)

Changes, Changes...
More Changes

We all change over the years. A student expressed shock one day
when I said my husband and I were celebrating our 31st wedding
anniversary. "How could you possibly stay with one person that
long?" she asked in amazement. My reply was that we each had lived
with several very different "people." As I told her, we each have changed
so much over the years that there hasn't been time to get bored.

The catch in such changes, of course, is that people may change in
different directions. "He's not at all like he was when I married
him." "She doesn't seem to care anymore." Rapid change in the
partner requires extra work and extra loving to keep a relationship
strong and caring.

Two Kinds of Changes

> *You asked if he changed. Well, he did for awhile. He thought*
> *he had me. He thought I had to do everything he asked me to do.*
> *After awhile we talked about it. I said, "Just because I'm with*
> *you doesn't mean I do everything you say."*
>
> *I think this happens a lot with young couples. When we were*
> *going together we went out all the time. We were never at*
> *home—plus I didn't have a baby. Now he takes me out only once*
> *in a great while. He thinks because we're married I'll stay home*
> *and watch TV.* (Arlene, married at 18 to Dale, 18)

Arlene is describing two kinds of changes. First, she felt her
husband had changed. In addition, their lifestyle changed from going
out a great deal to staying home much of the time.

Some people get married thinking that marriage will change a
partner—but only for the better. "After we're married he'll stop
drinking. He'll stop smoking and running around," she thinks.
However, Pati, married at 17 to Mike, 18, described a big change in
her husband before they were married:

> *I met Mike when I was 15. We were seeing each other for*
> *about two years before we got married. When I first met him he*
> *spent most of his time with his friends and his drinking. As a*
> *matter of fact, my in-laws thank me for getting him straightened*
> *out. When he met me he started spending more and more time*
> *with me instead of on the streets with his friends.*
>
> *I didn't want him to be the way he was when I first met him.*
> *He's much better now. I wouldn't be able to put up with him*

taking off with his friends while we're married. I realize now that he changed a lot before we got married. After the first six months we were together, he really calmed down. I think he realized he was getting into a lot of trouble and he needed a change.

Pati's story would probably have been quite different if she had married Mike *before* he changed, then had expected him to change *because* of their marriage. It's risky to think you can change someone else. The only person you can really change is yourself. Pati doesn't say she changed him—she says he decided to change, apparently because he wanted their relationship to work. Or was it because he grew up during that time?

Teenagers Change Faster

People usually change faster during their teenage years than they ever will again. Do you sometimes feel very mature, and at other times like a child? Are you feeling independent most of the time lately, but at times you want someone to take care of you? These are very normal feelings, especially among teenagers.

Such normal feelings, however, can make one a bit hard to live with. Your mother may be able to cope when, as she says, "You're acting like a child." But how will your partner react to such behavior?

When Lyle moved in we felt like we were playing house. He expected me to act older except he couldn't act older himself. He didn't want to go out and look for a job but he thought I should be sewing stuff for the baby and cooking for him. (Maralee, 16 when she lived with Lyle, also 16)

If you're starting married life with a baby, you may find it doubly hard. Many young women find they grow up fast during pregnancy. Sometimes their mates don't mature as quickly. "I feel like I have two babies," a young wife commented.

Being patient with each other is important. Encouraging each other to be the best person each of you can be will help. Time will help—as each of you grows older, you will probably grow more mature. It takes lots of self-discipline and lots of adjustment to learn to live with another person. If either or both of you are teenagers, it may take extra effort from both of you. But you can do it if you both work hard at succeeding together.

Changes After Marriage

You can be sure of one thing. Getting married and living together cause changes in one's life. About 360 teenagers who were either married or living with a partner completed the marriage attitudes survey. They answered several open-ended questions including "What do you feel you have given up because of your partnership?" The two Fs—freedom and friends—were mentioned much more often than anything else.

> *What did I give up? I gave up all my past—partying and going out. I put all that away. I wanted to dedicate myself to her. I don't think I would have wanted to settle down any sooner. A lot of people thought I was still too young, but I don't think so.* (Manuel, 20 when he lived with Darla, 16)

Many of the young people we interviewed spoke of changes in their life plans because of early marriage:

> *We grew up fast after Gloria got pregnant, and especially after we got married. I've had a job since tenth grade, and our parents were very supportive. We're very lucky that way, blessed. I knew they were there to help us and that took a lot of the burden off me.*
> *Our marriage did change some of my plans. If you had asked me about college the day before Gloria told me she was pregnant, I would have said yes. I was going, no doubt about it. I have always been good in math and I was leaning toward something like engineering. It did change my plans.* (Derek, married at 18 to Gloria, 18)

Only one-fifth of the teenagers in the marriage survey thought marriage would mean fewer friends. About 18 percent of the girls and fully one-quarter of the boys thought marriage would bring *more* friends. Yet many of the young marrieds reported loss of friends after marriage.

Cameron, 17, and Arlynne, 16, were both in high school when they married. Two years later he said:

> *Early marriage isn't really a good idea. You miss out on a lot like going out with your friends. I used to do a lot of things—I was gone from the house most of the time. I was always out some-where, and it's hard getting used to staying home all the time. Right now I'm beginning to get into doing things at home. I'm*

starting a dollhouse for the baby and making shelves for our apartment.

Arlynne added:

It's like I never had time to be independent. I went from being Mom's little girl to being a wife and mother. When I moved over here it was hard even though she lives right across the street. I'm constantly calling her, "Mom, what do I do? She's sick!"

Who Picks Up the Socks?

Living together brings obvious changes to a young couple's lifestyle. Perhaps you have had your own room all your life. Now you'll share it with your spouse. And the cleaning—for some people cleaning takes on added importance after marriage—or becomes more of a hassle.

Teenagers have a reputation for being messy. Parents have been known to call their son's or daughter's room "The Pigpen." Young people who delay marriage for several years after high school often learn how to get along with other adults through living together in a college dorm or moving into an apartment with friends. But one who moves directly from a parent's home into marriage may not realize the importance of compromise in daily living. One's partner may not be as willing to pick up after him/her as Mother was:

He's very messy and I'm not used to picking up after anybody but myself. He's from a family with four boys and his mom always picked up after him. I was on his back a lot at first. I'd like him to be neat.

When he takes his clothes off, he throws them on the floor. He leaves them there and they stack up. That's when I get upset. But he's getting better. (LeAnne, married at 17 to Colin, 20)

Some people have lived with a mother who always cleans up after them. When that person gets married, s/he may expect the other partner to do the picking up and the cleaning. Again, talk it through *before* you start living together.

If you know before you get married that both of you are fairly messy, you can do some planning together on coping. Will one of you pick up after the other? Or will each be responsible for his/her own mess? Will you take turns? Or...?

His Family—Her Family: Always Different

When two people from different families move in together, they
can't possibly have the same lives as they did before. Each family is
different. When you marry, you're combining two different
families—two ways of living. That takes lots of adjusting for both
partners.

One young wife was shocked to find her husband's mother cooked
beans in a different way than her mother did. To make it worse, her
husband thought his mother's beans tasted the best. His wife didn't
agree.

Tammy, 17, found it hard to cook because of the different foods
she and Rick, 18, were used to eating:

> There are a lot of foods that Rick doesn't like. I wasn't
> allowed to date until I was 16, so we didn't have much time to
> learn about each other's likes and dislikes.
> My mom made lots of things for us that he doesn't eat. It's hard to
> make out a menu, and that's why I didn't cook much in the beginning.

Perhaps Tammy and Rick can plan their meals together. She could
offer to fix some of his mother's dishes if he would agree to try some
of the foods she likes. Again, compromise should help.

Loneliness Versus Privacy

If someone who lives with a large family moves out into an apartment with a partner, s/he may miss the noise and bustle of a lot of
people coming and going. Alison, 15, married Paul, 20, in July, six
months before their baby was born. She remembers the loneliness:

> I didn't like it because I was alone. Paul didn't even like me on
> the phone or going anyplace. He didn't want me to waste time
> like that. Those six months until Billie was born were the loneliest
> of my life. We didn't have furniture and I spent most of the time
> sitting on the rug in front of the TV.

Yvette, 17, was a senior in high school when she and Vince, 19,
were married. She, too, missed her family:

> That first week I just wanted to come back to my mom. I said,
> "Oh, this is terrible. I miss my mom." He said, "You have to get

used to it, to being alone." He was working nights and I only
had him in the morning. It was so lonely I would cry. We were
living in another town and I didn't know anybody. I would call
my mom and ask her to come over. It's hard at first getting used
to that life, to being alone.

Other people find they don't have enough time alone after they get
married:

*Privacy? That was real strange. I had lived alone for several
months, and I thought I would go crazy after Kent moved in.
This guy was always here. I missed things like being able to read
a book with the TV off. And sports—every woman should find
out about that before she moves in with a man...find out if he
likes sports. If he does and you don't, get another TV!* (Amy,
married at 19 to Kent, also 19)

Change Is Inevitable

Change within a relationship is inevitable. Some change is good,
some not so good. If the partners in their changing go in different
directions, their relationship may suffer.

Much of the secret to changing together lies in good communication.
If two people who love and care for each other can talk together
about the changes going on in their lives, they can continue to grow
together. They may find 30 years from now that each is an entirely
different person—but that their love for each other has grown even
stronger and more caring through these changes.

Two people working toward this goal are likely to be winners in the
search for a loving, caring, long-lasting relationship.

Chapter 4

*Do communicate. Don't let some-
thing boil into a big argument.
Don't think it'll disappear—it won't.
It just grows and grows. When we
argue he'll either come to me or I'll
go to him and say, "Let's talk this
out," and from there we'll take it
on. "OK, you don't like this. What
do you want me to do about it?"*

*Sometimes we'll be talking and he
says, "You should have told me."
"Well, I'm telling you now."*

(Marcella, married eight years ago at 15
to Walt, 19)

Creative
Communication

*Fights? Lloyd won't even talk to me. All I can do is wait until
he's ready to talk again and pretend like nothing ever happened. I
have to wait until it blows over which is very annoying to me. I
find myself doing all the talking most of the time when we're
arguing about something. Lloyd is a very stubborn, hardheaded
person and he likes things his own way. I can't stand it because
he won't talk.* (Elaine, married at 16 to Lloyd, 17)

*Communication—that's what I liked about him when I first
started seeing him. He was easy to talk to. We have our little
fights—everybody does—but we sit down and talk them over and
that helps. At first we're mad at each other, then we won't speak
for awhile. Then we start talking about it.* (Pati, 17, married to
Mike, 18)

Nearly 250 married and/or living-together teenagers answered the
question, "What are the biggest problems in your partnership?" Most
often mentioned were money problems. Communication received the
next highest number of votes as a problem-causer. No matter what
their age, many couples worry about the lack of communication
between them.

Nearly every young couple I talked with stressed the importance of
good communication in a relationship. Over and over they said,
"You've got to talk things out. You've got to share your feelings."

Mixed Messages Cause Problems

Fred, 20, a very perceptive young man, spoke of his concern with
the mixed messages he was receiving from Peggy, 19. They've been
married a year and, even though they both speak English, they aren't
understanding each other. He said:

*I think the exciting thing about going to a marriage counselor
must be having someone sitting there listening to us both, then
translating what we say into the other's language.*

*For example, a friend of mine recently drove our car to the
store for some beer. He'd been drinking a little, and he almost
had an accident right here in front of our house. We were
lucky—he pulled out of it in time.*

*When Peggy brought it up later, I thought she was attacking
me, saying my friend was stupid and shouldn't ever be allowed to
drive. That wasn't what she said, but that's what I heard.*

> *I realize now she was saying, "We worked hard for that car and we need it to get to work. If it's wrecked, we have a big problem. Let's don't loan it to him again."*
>
> *It was a big hassle. Instead of taking comments like this personally, I need to find a way to understand her more clearly. I guess I could have listened better.*

Yes, Fred probably could have listened better. Peggy perhaps could have chosen a better way to express herself. She might have said, "I feel worried when Jasper drives our car because I don't think he's a safe driver." Fred could have replied, "I think you're worried about Jasper driving our car."

If she agrees this is her "message," they can then discuss a solution. Perhaps in the future one of them will agree to drive Jasper to the store. Or perhaps they'll set up a simple "No one else drives our car" rule. Whatever the solution, it should be easier to find once both partners understand the problem. The result could be one less problem between Fred and Peggy.

One of the big breakdowns in communication happens during the receiving. One person says one thing, the other hears something else. A question as simple as "What's for dinner?" could mean several different things: "Is dinner ready yet or shall I go to the bathroom first?" or "I'm starving—let's eat." The person receiving the "What's for dinner?" message might hear something entirely different: "You must not be very efficient if dinner isn't ready yet" or "I hope we're not having tuna casserole again." Simple feedback could be, "You're afraid we're having tuna casserole again?" or "I feel you're being critical because dinner isn't ready." This gives him an opportunity either to agree or to send his message again, perhaps in a different way.

If He Won't Talk

Several young people described silent mates, partners who refuse to discuss. In our culture, the male is likely to have a harder time expressing his feelings. From infancy, little girls are talked to more than boys. Girls are encouraged to show their feelings while boys are expected to "act like a man." Boys aren't supposed to cry. In fact, the "strong silent type" is often considered a positive label.

The marriage attitudes survey included the question, "If you are upset with your partner, what do you do?" Almost two-thirds of the girls said they would tell their partners they were upset. Far fewer of

the boys—about half—gave this answer. Almost 30 percent of the
boys said they would leave and think it through. Not as many girls
gave this response.

Strangely enough, almost four times as many boys as girls responded
that the male should usually have the final say in an argument. If many
women say their men won't talk, yet these men feel they should have
the final say, trouble is brewing. It's not a partnership if one person
does the talking while the other makes the decisions.

Annie, 15 when she married Jose, 17, was often frustrated because
Jose wouldn't argue. He refused to discuss their problems:

> *He always takes off and I always want him to stay here so we
> can talk about it. But he doesn't want to talk, so he leaves. When
> he comes back, I make him listen to me.*
>
> *Sometimes if I know we're going to be arguing, I hide the car
> keys until it's time for him to go to work the next day. Then he
> doesn't go very far. For awhile it makes things worse, but I just
> keep talking to him. Finally he comes around and listens to me.*
>
> *Usually he walks around the house and tries to ignore me, but I
> follow him around and talk to him. Eventually he does start
> talking. I don't know whether this helps, but it's the only way I
> can get him to listen to me.*

Annie's problem is shared by many people. However, there must be
a better solution than hiding the car keys. If your partner will talk
willingly, you're much better off than if you try to force the issue.

Reasons for Not Talking

Why won't Jose talk to his wife? There may be several reasons.
Perhaps he has never learned how to share with other people.
Arlynne, 16, and Cameron, 17, discussed this situation:

> Cameron: *I have a problem with that. At home I hide my
> emotions. It's just the way I've been. I keep asking Arlynne not
> to ask so many questions, to quit saying, "What's wrong? What
> are you thinking?" I don't know how to answer her.*
>
> Arlynne: *He's been by himself so there's been no reason to talk
> about things. But in my family we talked things out. When he
> won't tell me what's wrong, it makes me so mad. Sometimes it
> gets the whole situation out of hand and we'll start fighting about*

something entirely different. I'm so mad at him for not talking that I'll say something I don't really want to say. Then he gets mad.

Marvin Greenbaum, clinical psychologist in Portland, Oregon, has an interesting viewpoint on the importance of lots of talking between partners. "I think it's overvalued," he said bluntly. "Sometimes trying to communicate to your partner *everything* you're feeling simply adds more pressure to your relationship.

"Maybe it's like sex," he continued. "They say a couple with a good sexual relationship considers sex about 25 percent of their total relationship. But if a couple has a lousy time in bed, they think sex should be about 90 percent of the marriage.

"For many people, communication is a lot like that. If you have it, it's not a big deal. But if you don't...that's when the importance of communication may be over-emphasized.

"A lot of young couples say you've got to be honest, you must tell people how you feel. But this can have two effects," Dr. Greenbaum explained. "First, it adds a lot of pressure to their relationship. Second, there's an inequality there because girls are generally better at communicating than boys are. I see people expecting too much out of communication. Sure, it's an important part of marriage, but it doesn't offer a magic formula for happiness forever."

We need to remember that communication between people can happen without words. Fred explained:

> *Peggy wants to talk all the time. She thinks we're not sharing our lives if we don't talk about everything we do. I can sit on the porch with her beside me and read for two hours and feel close. She thinks we've got to talk or we're not communicating.*

Plan Time to Talk

Sometimes people won't talk because they don't think they have anything to offer. Or they may feel talking won't change anything so why bother? Often a person may be afraid to express him/herself for fear of being rejected.

If your partner doesn't respond when you're ready to argue, think about how you communicate the rest of the time. Does s/he share feelings, dreams, frustrations with you? Would you like to talk more?

There are lots of ways *not* to communicate with your partner. Leaving the TV on discourages talking. So does reading the paper during dinner. Always being busy with the kids or with projects in the garage reduces opportunities to talk with one's spouse.

One way to work on this problem is to plan special times you can talk together. Maybe you'll take a walk together or have a romantic dinner by candlelight. Some couples find they talk more freely when they're eating out. If you have children, plan some time with your spouse *without* the kids.

Let the silent partner choose the time to talk. When he does, LISTEN! Show that you're willing to accept feelings and frustrations. This doesn't mean you always have to agree with him. But if he finds you really do listen and you obviously care, he may find it easier to talk with you. You need to know what's going on inside your partner's mind and s/he needs to have some idea of what you're thinking.

> *We usually have good communication but it started getting real bad recently. I finally told Jeff, "I don't want it to be like this anymore." So we sat down and I told him what was bugging me and he told me what was bugging him.*
>
> *Like while his dad was here—he hadn't seen him in two years, and it was real strange—it was just like it was him and his dad only. I told Jeff I was feeling left out. I could understand if we were just boyfriend-girlfriend, but I'm his wife. Jeff was*

*uncomfortable with me in bed even—because his dad was in the
next room. I told him we're married, we weren't doing anything
wrong. Talking about it helped.* (Joni, married at 15 to Jeff, 18)

Some people find a good communication starter is to write their
feelings down, then share that with the other person. Heather, married
at 17 to Delbert, 16, said:

*When we couldn't talk, I'd write him letters. At first, I wasn't
writing the letters to him, just about him and my feelings about
the situation. Then one time he found one and said, "What's
this?" I said, "No, you can't read that." He said, "Why not?" I
finally let him read it. He got kind of teary-eyed about it, and I
think he understood my feelings better than he ever had before.*

Sometimes expressing one's feelings in writing makes those feelings
somehow more real to the person reading about them. And some
people can express their feelings better through writing than by talking.

*That was a bad scene last summer. Everything had been
building up for several months, and I let go. I blew, telling him
everything I didn't like about our lives. He acted like he didn't
even care. I went over to my girlfriend's house for two days.
When I came home he was here with a long letter saying he was
sorry for the way he acted and he would try to do better. He said
he didn't know why he did the things he did, but he would have
to work it out somehow. That helped a lot.*

*Lloyd can write his feelings down on paper much easier than he
can tell me. There are things on paper that you wouldn't think
came out of Lloyd.* (Elaine)

Handling Arguments

There is some conflict in every marriage. No two people agree on
everything all the time. Rebecca and Jason, married when they were
17 and 21, were divorced within two years. She said:

*Jason and I never argued and I'm sure that was our downfall.
Now I can appreciate a good argument. It's unrealistic to think
that two people can agree on everything. No two people are going
to feel the same all the time, and I know now it's OK to disagree.*

> *We got married and figured we didn't have to worry about this*
> *relationship. But that didn't work.*

When you do argue, attack the problem, not each other. And stay in the present. Learn to forget what happened yesterday when you're discussing today's problems. Stay on the subject—and don't put down your partner's relatives!

When you're expressing your feelings, keep to the I-messages. Instead of saying, "Where have you been all evening?" try "I was worried (or lonely or...) because you weren't here tonight." Instead of saying, "You're spending too much money," try "I'm terribly concerned because we can't pay our bills. I'd like to do something about it."

Chances are that your partner will respond cooperatively to your I-messages. Being put on the defensive is a waste of time. That's what you do to her/him when you accuse. An I-message is likely to lead into a problem-solving conversation.

Questions to Ask Yourself

A good question to ask yourself when you feel a fight brewing is "Is this issue worth fighting over?" It took Jean and Dick awhile to understand this point:

> *Our arguments are mild now. When we first got married we*
> *fought over every little thing, stupid things. After awhile you*
> *forget what you're fighting about. Now we each overlook things*
> *more. I think you have to—you can't pick on every little detail.*
> (Jean, married at 16 to Dick, 18)

When you argue about something, try asking yourself these questions: What do I want to gain out of this discussion? What does my spouse want? What will I have to do in order to satisfy my needs and my partner's needs in this area? Hopefully, your partner is asking him/herself the same questions.

If it is "your" issue, state your case clearly, then ask for feedback. Listen to your partner's feedback. You'll learn whether s/he really heard you or not. Then respond to the feedback.

This is when so many people bring in other issues, but it's important to stick to the subject. Always remember to attack the problem, not each other.

> *You have to learn to separate what you're arguing about right then from your love and your life. You can't let a stupid little thing ruin things. We used to fight real bad, and then we realized it wasn't worth all that. Now when we fight it's over something that matters.* (Kent, married at 19 to Amy, 19)

If you criticize, offer solutions. If you don't think the two of you have enough money, for example, what can you do to improve the situation? Can you go to work or get a better job? What can you do to cut down on expenses? Sometimes you may be able to get your partner to brainstorm solutions with you.

In brainstorming, each of you will think of all kinds of possible solutions to a problem. Your ideas don't all have to make sense. The important thing is to get lots of ideas out there to examine. Basic rule of a brainstorming session is that neither of you criticizes the ideas offered by the other.

Jean and Dick solved a possible problem rather simply by looking at a couple of alternatives and making a choice together:

> *On his 21st birthday he asked if it would be OK with me if he went out to a bar. Of course I told him to go ahead. But then he wanted to make it a habit.*
>
> *We didn't really fight about it, we just talked. I asked him if he wanted me to go there after I turn 21 in two years. He said, "No, I guess not." He doesn't go to the bar anymore. He brings his friends over here because he knows I'd rather have them here than have him over there.*

When you're arguing, realize that "You never" or "You always" aren't allowed! "You never take out the trash," "You always nag me about that" are not helpful comments. Is your goal to have a closer relationship with your mate and to solve problems in the process? Then try to avoid putting your partner down with such accusations.

Bob and Jean Bayard, psychologists and authors of *How to Deal with Your Acting-Up Teenager* (1983: Evans), talked about the "ping-pong" method of communication. She says, "You're no good." He says, "You're no good, either." She says...and on they go, passing insults back and forth like a ping-pong ball.

"It only takes one person to stop playing this game," Dr. Jean Bayard said. "If he calls me names and I say, 'I really feel hurt right now,' there's no way for him to hit back." Try it the next time you and your partner start a verbal ping-pong game.

Dealing With Anger

No matter how much you try to stick to the subject and how intently you listen to your partner, sometimes you're going to be angry. Expressing anger is OK. People who constantly bury their anger tend to have stomachaches.

> *We yell and scream at each other. Screaming gets the initial thing off your chest. Then we go back and talk about it. Why do you go out all the time? Why don't you take me out? Why don't you do the dishes? He doesn't say much of anything—he keeps most of it inside which is bad. I don't know what's eating him until he talks.* (Elise, married at 18 to Hector, 20)

When you're furious, however, you may say things you don't even mean, things that are hurtful to your partner. An approach which may help is sharing your feelings early in the discussion. Say "I'm getting angry." But don't accuse—don't say, "You're making me angry."

Sometimes it may help to say, "Let's stop this discussion for now. I'm saying things I really don't mean and I don't want this to happen.

Let's talk about it tomorrow." This is a big order if you're really angry. Or you might try Dale's approach:

> *Dale's dad was into hitting his mother. I think he tries to be calm with me when we argue because he knows he doesn't want that. But lots of times he'll get mad—and then he'll sit down and he'll actually count, 1-2-3-4. Then he'll say, "Well, I'm ready to talk." Sometimes it makes me laugh and that stops the whole argument.* (Arlene, married at 18 to Dale, 18)

Couples who can get a little humor into their arguments will find it's harder to stay angry. Arlene continued:

> *Sometimes when I get mad, I look in the mirror at myself and I start laughing. Chrissie stops us a lot too. When she's here, she'll say, "No, stop that." We know it's not good anyway for a child to see you arguing back and forth. Here Chrissie at 3 years old stands there and says, "No." That makes us laugh too.*

Several couples mentioned following the rule, "Don't go to sleep on your anger." This is included in the "Rules for a Happy Marriage" which Derek and Gloria hung on their bedroom wall. It's important even if you've been fighting, always to kiss each other good-night.

"Don't hit and run away" is another good rule for dealing with arguments. Laying all your frustrations out on your partner, then walking away saying, "I don't want to talk about it anymore," isn't playing fair. You don't solve anything by saying your piece, then stopping the conversation.

Just as frustrating is the partner who hears you out, then refuses to respond. Again, "I don't want to talk about it" or, even worse, a cold silence solves nothing.

> *Two years after my divorce I married Don. He tends to blow up, then wants to forget it. But I've gotten to the point where I'm not going to be walked on. As soon as he's done, I talk out my feelings. He thinks about what I say and I think about what he says. Neither of us likes to argue, but we know sometimes it's necessary.* (Rebecca, married at 21 to Don, 25)

Once you and your partner have discussed your problem, however, and found a solution, then by all means drop it. Bringing up yesterday's argument is an emotional waste for both of you.

Have you heard the term "gunnysacking"? This refers to storing up lots of complaints—putting them in the "gunnysack"—then dumping them on the other person all at once. It's a bad scene anytime, but you can be sure it won't help a marriage relationship. Again, when you're arguing, stick to the subject rather than bringing in a bunch of other complaints.

"Wish List" Approach

One approach to solving problems would be for each person to write down an "I wish" list, as suggested by Dr. Carlfred Broderick in *Couples* (1981: Simon and Schuster). Each one makes out an "I wish you would" list. Make each "I wish" something specific that could possibly be changed. Then compare lists and negotiate.

He might write:
1. I wish you would quit complaining when I go out with my friends.
2. I wish you wouldn't visit your mother so often.
3. I wish you'd keep the house cleaner.

Her list might be:
1. I wish you'd put the baby to bed at night.
2. I wish you would pick up after yourself.
3. I wish you would stay home more.

Negotiating means each gives a little. Can they each offer to satisfy one of the other's wishes? Perhaps she'll keep the house cleaner if he'll pick up after himself. If he bathes the baby, she'll have time to clean up the kitchen. Or she might say she'll quit nagging him about going out with his friends if he'll bathe the baby before he leaves.

Wish lists are a good place to start when you're looking for compromise solutions to your problems. Remember that it's important to stay on the subject when you're discussing these lists. Be positive, and don't turn it into another session in which each of you criticizes the other unmercifully.

When you're discussing your list or anything else, stick to expressing your own feelings. Don't evaluate or criticize your partner. That almost never solves anything. It's important that you take responsibility for solving your own problems.

Perhaps your partner seems always to be bad-tempered, inconsiderate, and abusive. If so, Dr. Broderick suggests that you be positive every time you can for at least three weeks. You may find your partner's disposition improves.

Different Family Scripts

Most disagreements have no absolute right and wrong. You'll see an incident differently than your partner sees it. Often what seems to be a big problem can be understood by looking at the "life scripts" each of you brought into your relationship.

In her family, perhaps Dad did the laundry while Mother cooked. In his family, Mother did both, but she didn't have an outside job. Each partner may feel strongly that there is only one "right" way to run a home—and often that is based on the way s/he grew up.

In fact, the way you communicate is likely to be much like your parents' ways. You and your partner may very well be scripted into communicating in quite different ways. If this is true, you'll need to work hard at learning to understand each other.

You may do most of your communicating with words. To you, words may be all-important. You can express your feelings and your frustrations. You're willing to talk about whatever is on your mind. Verbal communication is no problem for you.

Your partner may have grown up in a family where people didn't talk much. They didn't express their feelings through words. If each of you is tolerant and understanding of the other's ways, the situation will probably improve as it did for Elise and Hector:

> *That's the most important thing, communication. We're developing more over the years. At first Hector was very inward. He wouldn't talk about anything. But as the years go on, I see him breaking up a little and able to talk to me about problems. Maybe he's gaining more trust in me, knowing maybe I can help him with his problems. He doesn't have to keep them to himself.* (Elise)

Communication is when something is going on inside you and you give that to the other person. Expressing your own feelings and learning to listen to the other person are necessary for good communication to occur. Good communication is a basic part of a good relationship.

Chapter 5

> When we got married, it was scary.
> It was different... all of a sudden
> Jimmy was in my room. It was
> awkward having my parents outside
> the door. That was one of our
> problems while we were living
> there—sex. The walls weren't made
> of brick. We lived there two years
> and we coped. But it's better now
> that we have our own apartment.

(Lauri, married at 17 to Jimmy, 18)

Sex Begins In The Kitchen

Sex Begins in the Kitchen is the title of a book by Dr. Kevin Leman (1981: Regal Books). Contrary to what you may be thinking, Dr. Leman is not suggesting you and your spouse should necessarily make love regularly on the kitchen floor. Instead he writes about the importance of your total relationship and of its effect on your sexual relationship.

Effect of Total Relationship

How you and your spouse react to each other in bed is closely tied to how you act with each other the rest of the time. Consider the amount of time you actually spend in preparation for and having sexual intercourse. If you're a highly sexed couple, this may be several hours each week. But even if it's one hour each day, that leaves 161 hours weekly for other activities. And most people spend much less than seven hours per week "having" sex.

How a couple treats each other during those 161-plus hours greatly influences their love-making. If she nags him every day about their terrible apartment and the fact that he makes very little money, he won't feel as loving as he might otherwise. If he puts her down constantly or if he's "out with the boys" several nights a week, she may not be thrilled about having sex with him.

Often, couples with sexual problems find, if they work at solving other problems in their lives, their sex life will also improve. Our sexuality is not a separate thing existing somehow only in our genitals. It's part of us in the same way our minds and our emotions are part of us.

Communication is a vital part of any good relationship. That communication is important in developing a good sexual relationship. Find out what you and your partner already know about the sexuality of men and women. You may want to choose a good book on the subject, and learn or refresh your knowledge together. One excellent choice is *Teenage Body Book* by Kathy McCoy and Charles Wibbelsman (1979: Pocket Books).

How Important Is Sex?

About half the young people in the marriage attitudes survey thought each spouse should be a good sex partner. Another third thought this was somewhat important. Interestingly, young women who already had a child tended to think being a good sex partner was less important for either the husband or wife. Those who were pregnant put even less importance on this characteristic.

People vary a great deal in how much or how often they prefer to have intercourse. If both consider sex a very important part of their lives and want to "do it" twice a day, that's fine. If neither thinks sex is all that important, and they don't get around to having intercourse very often, that's OK too.

> *My mom tells me, "It's real weird how you guys never do nothing." When we were living by ourselves we used to do stuff together, like in bed. A friend said the other day that she never sees us kiss, and we don't. It takes about a month before we do something in bed.*
>
> *Some people, they have to have it, and some people really don't care. Like me and him, it don't really bug us. It's only natural for a guy to want it once in awhile, but it's not an every-day thing—just once in awhile.* (Estella, married at 18 to Joel, 20)

Estella and Joel apparently have a satisfactory relationship. I do wonder about the meaning of "When we were living by ourselves..." The lack of privacy apparently has changed their sex life. The reassuring thing is that they seem to agree on this important topic. Problems are more likely to occur if one person wants to make love every night while the other one is usually "too tired."

> *We have problems with sex because he wants it every day while once a month is fine for me. I guess sex is pretty important.* (Melodie, married at 17 to Brett, 19)

Talk and Compromise Are Essential

If you disagree in other areas of your relationship, talk and compromise are important. Talk and compromise are just as important in disagreements over sex. However, there are some added complications with sex. It's hard for most people to accept a turn down from a spouse in the bedroom.

If one's mate doesn't want eggs for breakfast, it's usually no big deal. But if that same mate, after love-making is started, says, "No, I'm not in the mood," the other person is likely to feel rejected.

Somehow in our society we have this myth of both men and women being constantly ready for sex. If you don't believe it, watch the TV soap operas.

On the other hand, women, especially, are learning that it is important not to fake an interest in sex just to please a man. Sex should *not* be a "should," something that one does because one is expected to. It's OK to say, "Not this time."

Do these two paragraphs seem to be saying two entirely different things? According to the first one, we should never say, "No." But the next paragraph says, "It's OK to say 'No'." Loving and caring partners need to work out their own approach based on these two ideas. It's important not to make your partner feel rejected. It's also important not to force yourself to have sex if you don't want to.

The answer lies in compromise, in both partners considering the feelings of both, and in working out answers for their own situation.

In sex as in anything else, it's easy to blame the other person. "It's her fault if I don't achieve great heights of sexual pleasure." "If he knew what he was doing, I'd like it." Blaming someone else doesn't change anything. Talking together about what feels good to each of you might help. And remind each other that a good sexual relationship takes time.

If one partner finds s/he is usually the one most interested in sex (among teenagers, this more often is the male), placing more attention on the desires of the other is very important. If she isn't as interested in sex as he would like, they need to learn to communicate their feelings about what feels good to each one. Caressing, intimacy, touching, and kissing are important—more important than intercourse to some people.

Conflict of Expectations

Ellen Peach, family nurse practitioner, Community Health Clinics, Inc., Nampa, Idaho, talks about the different expectations men and women often have for each other. "Sometimes this is because of lack of experience with themselves and their own sexuality and of the sexuality of the opposite sex," she said. "They don't have a good understanding of male and female arousal, of what turns people on.

"Different people feel comfortable with different things, and you both need to work that out in your relationship. This means you have to talk to each other about what brings pleasure to each of you. It's important that neither exploit the other by doing something that makes the other person uncomfortable.

"A good sexual relationship is a good talking relationship," she continued. "It's important that they talk often about their wants. Only in this way can they understand they aren't always going to have the same needs. Lots of times, if there is mutual respect and caring, compromise can occur."

Other Problems with Sex

Just as good sex depends on a good relationship in other parts of your life, so can problems which affect your sex life cause problems in other ways:

> *We're having sexual problems now. I have a yeast infection and I've had it for several months. We thought it was cured, and we'd start to have sex. Then we couldn't because it would burn. I'm still going to the doctor.*
>
> *There's a lot of pressure, fighting over little things because of that. Colin always says, "Well, I can live without that. I don't care." But it is a problem. It isn't a big part of our life, but it certainly is there.* (LeAnne, married at 17 to Colin, 20)

When something like this happens, be sure you get good medical care. If you and your partner have been able to talk about anything and everything including your feelings about sex, you'll be able to cope with this kind of problem. Colin apparently understands that intercourse is not fun or even comfortable for LeAnne while she has this infection. He's trying to be as reassuring to her as possible.

Elaine, married at 16 to Lloyd, 17, voiced a worry felt by many people, young and old, when she said:

> *A lot of people think sex is important, and I agree. Sex is very important. If you aren't compatible in your sex life, he or she will go out and find it someplace else.*

But infidelity is usually not so much a search for sex as it is a search for emotional intimacy or ego boosting. If a couple can face this fact and do something about it, they are likely to stay together. They are also likely to grow closer to each other.

Good Relationship Takes Time

It is super-important to remember that a good sex relationship usually takes time to develop. The custom of waiting until after marriage for sex, but expecting it to be wonderful on the wedding night when both people are exhausted, is not very realistic. Neither is it realistic to expect sex to be the best if the couple can't count on enough privacy or if they must rush through their lovemaking.

Learning to know each other, being able to talk about all parts of their partnership including the sexual part, and having plenty of time to experience each other can add up to a satisfying relationship. But this doesn't happen overnight. *Good sex takes time.*

Apparently some teenage women don't like sex much. Often I have heard someone say it's something you "do" for men. Sometimes a discussion of sex turns into a discussion of how to get out of sex.

How did you learn about sex? Did you grow up thinking sex was dirty, something not at all nice? Did/Do you think of your parents as sexual beings? Young people sometimes tell me that of course their parents don't do "that" anymore. Ideas like these influence our attitudes toward our own sexuality. Many of us have a lot of unlearning to do in order to grow into a happy, satisfying sexual relationship with another person.

The fear of pregnancy can keep a woman from enjoying sex. She and her partner need to select a reliable method of birth control and use it *every* time they have intercourse. If they do, she is likely to become more interested in sex.

Effects of Guilt Feelings

If you're feeling guilty about this relationship, that it isn't right to be having sex at this time, this undoubtedly influences your feelings. There are good reasons why many people think sex is OK only within marriage. However, if sex is supposed to be good after the wedding, it's hard to understand why it was bad the day before. It's hard to change one's feelings that quickly.

Donita and Ray were married during their senior year of high school. Donita remembers:

> That first week felt weird. I remember lying in bed and thinking, "Just a piece of paper makes it OK." It's strange how people think it's OK now if you're in bed together but if you didn't have that piece of paper, it wasn't right before. It's OK that kids come in and see us lying together. But it would not be OK if they saw my sister in bed with her boyfriend.

The point here is not whether or not couples should have sex before marriage. The point is that if you are in a sexual relationship with someone, a relationship that you consider good and you want to continue, you're making it hard for yourself if you can't think and talk openly with your partner about the subject.

If you have a child, you can help her/him grow up realizing that we are all sexual people. Sex is not supposed to be dirty or bad. A person can use sex to hurt someone else, but that's not the kind of person you want your child to be.

The double standard is still with us—the idea that sex is OK for boys, whether married or not, but it isn't really OK for girls. You can help your child, whether a boy or girl, to grow up to be a caring, loving person who will be able to develop a healthy and satisfying sexual relationship with another person at the "right" time.

Childbirth and Sexual Feelings

Ms. Peach talked about the effect of childbirth on a woman's sex drive. "He may find it hard to understand why Mom is so tired and beat. A lot of 18-year-old guys want to hop in the sack two weeks after childbirth—but she's interested only in a little cuddling. Her sex drive is probably very low, quite different from his at this time. Sometimes it's hard to work these things out."

Mary Jane, married when she was 16 to Carl, 18, was talking two months after their twin daughters were born:

> *I just don't feel very sexy. This makes Carl mad. He says that I don't love him, but that's ridiculous. Of course I love him. But I don't feel like having sex.*
>
> *Twice we've gotten a sitter to take the girls out for a couple of hours. I felt different then. That was really nice.*

Mary Jane is undoubtedly exhausted. Taking care of one baby is more than enough for most people, but twins? Sometimes hiring a babysitter and sending that person *out* with the baby can do great things for a couple's relationship.

Fear of getting pregnant again can make one feel very unsexy. Breastfeeding can't be relied on to keep you from having another baby. A condom and foam used together provide a good method until you talk with your doctor or go to a family planning clinic.

Pain during lovemaking is a real problem for many new mothers, especially if they had stitches after delivery. If she's afraid sex will hurt, she'll feel anxious. That can start a vicious circle because anxiety and tension make it worse.

Some women have vaginal dryness if they're breastfeeding. This may make intercourse painful, or at least uncomfortable. Using a water-base lubricant such as K-Y Jelly should help.

Saying "No" is, of course, everyone's right. If a woman has just had a baby, she probably isn't particularly interested in sex. Her doctor may suggest she wait at least a month, perhaps six weeks, before having intercourse again. Even then she may find it uncomfortable.

If both partners love and want to please each other, they'll talk about their feelings. They'll share their thinking whether it's "I'm feeling terribly horny right now" or "This baby has made me so tired that the last thing I want to think about is sex." If both of you truly listen to each other, you'll find caring solutions that work OK for both of you.

This, Too, Will Pass

Jean Brunelli, nurse in the Tracy Infant Center, Cerritos, California, talked about this situation. "I know this can become a problem with young couples. Of course we support the young

mother's right not to feel sexy after childbirth. We also need to
remember that young guys talk a lot about sex and feel very
competitive. They like to brag about their sexual prowess. At the same
time, this young man is being turned away by his woman, which may
actually make him feel abnormal. He can't get her to do it when
everybody else is doing it all the time."

> *He has a hard time understanding how you feel when you're*
> *pregnant and after the baby is born—why you don't want to have*
> *sex all the time. He doesn't understand why you get upset real*
> *easy, why you cry over nothing. We talk about it a lot. We can*
> *communicate. But it's hard.* (Melodie)

"There is no simple solution. Best thing is for the young couple to
talk about it," Ms. Brunelli continued. "He should be able to say to
her, 'It makes me feel weird. Every guy I know seems to be having sex
all the time. Why can't we?' Maybe she needs to be able to say, 'This
is just a short time in our lives. It's a part of the whole experience of
having a baby. This will change.'

"If they're able to have some time alone and if she gets more rest,
this stage should end more quickly," Ms. Brunelli concluded.

If you and your partner have not had a baby yet, be aware that
these problems may occur. Before your baby is born is a time when
you probably will feel very close and warm, and you won't yet have
the distractions of constant babycare. This is the best time to start
talking about how you'll handle the pressures that almost always
occur after delivery.

Ms. Brunelli also talked about the other pressures young fathers
may be feeling. "Perhaps a few months ago his paycheck was
supposed to support himself and his car. Now with that same
paycheck he's trying to support his wife and child. This often causes a
lot of stress. Many young men look at sex as a stress reducer, and if
they can't do that, they're really puzzled," she added.

A wonderful book, *Pajamas Don't Matter* by Trish Gribben (1980:
Jalmar Press), is mostly a babycare book. But it also contains a two-
page section, "When Sex Turns You Off." Ms. Gribben talks about
the fact that it's absolutely normal for mothers to lose their interest in
sex for awhile after childbirth. She may not want intercourse for a few
weeks, or perhaps a longer time. Often a woman who feels like this
gets upset when her spouse touches her or kisses her. She thinks it
must be the beginning of making love when all she wants right then is
a feeling of closeness.

"If you're having a bad time in bed, don't think you're on your own," Ms. Gribben writes (p. 48). "It's a very common scene but it's not part of life and loving that many people are prepared for."

Before there were just two of us. Now there's the baby. If we're doing something and the baby cries, one of us has to get up. That's a real turn off. (Marcie, married at 15 to Elwood, 16)

There is nothing quite like a crying baby to ruin a romantic moment. At such times, a sense of humor may save the day—or night, as the case may be.

Sharing Baby Care Helps

Incidentally, this may be another reason for Dad to get involved in parenting his infant. Parenting at this stage means getting up night after night with the baby, changing diapers time after time, rocking her, talking to her, loving her, feeding her. Dad can play a full-parent role in everything except breastfeeding.

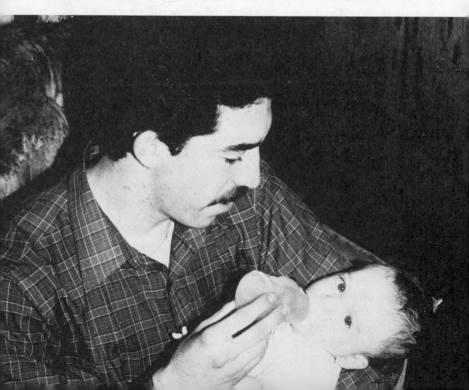

If he's acting like a parent—which means not expecting Mother to do all the work with the baby—he may find a bonus. Mother is much more likely to be interested in sex sooner than she would be if she were responsible for all the tremendous amount of work associated with taking care of a tiny infant.

Sex Is Not a Competition

Slang for the sex act generally is not very positive. Competition— "Did you score?" "I didn't even get to first base"—is often stressed in the way we talk about sex. In a competitive sport, Dr. Leman says in *Sex Begins in the Kitchen*, there is an attitude of superior/inferior relationships. Somebody has to win and somebody has to lose.

But if sex is going to be satisfying to a couple, it will not be at all like competitive sports. It will be a cooperative venture, a time when two people can work/play together and enjoy each other with no thought of one being inferior or superior to the other.

Men and women are, however, different in more than the fact that one has a penis, the other, a vagina. Most men are turned on faster than women. For most men, intercourse is the most important thing. For many women, the hugging and cuddling is at least as important as the sex act itself.

If either you or your partner grew up thinking sex is ugly and disgusting, you may find it harder to have a satisfactory sexual relationship. If one partner feels relaxed and good about sexual activities, s/he may be able to help her/his spouse become more comfortable with the subject.

This book is not meant to be a sex manual. If you want specific help with sex problems, there are some good books available. If you think your problems are too big to solve yourselves, you may decide to see a therapist. Ask your doctor or call your local mental health clinic for recommendations.

And always remember—Sex begins in the kitchen!

Chapter 6

*I clean toilets. She works, she fixes
the car. We both look after the kids.*

*I used to say "I'm not going to
wash no dishes, I'll throw out the
trash, I'll do the yard, but I won't
wash no dishes." But she taught me a
lot of things. We share our lives now.*

(Ruben, married at 20 to Shari, 19)

Roles...
His Job Or Hers?

Traditional roles? Yes, he says that's the normal way to do it. But there are many times I wish he would do the laundry or the ironing. In fact, I got to the place where I don't do the ironing. I just put his in the closet. If he wants it, he irons it.

He still won't do dishes unless I ask him and he happens to be in the mood. He rarely watches the kids. He's home Fridays and could save us the babysitting money, but he won't. He does take out the trash, fix the cars, and take care of the yard.

We don't talk about it much—that I want help with the laundry. He says, "If you didn't work, you wouldn't need my help." He'd like me to quit work, and then he'd want a spotless house. I couldn't do that. Besides, we need my paycheck, too, to pay our bills. (Elise, married five years ago to Hector. She was 18, he was 20.)

Who does the dishes in your home? Mows the lawn? Repairs the car? Vacuums the rug? Feeds and diapers the baby?

Until recently, such questions had easy answers. In most homes, the woman took care of the house while the man was likely to be in charge of the car and the yard.

This used to be a workable arrangement for many people. The man was supposed to earn the living. He was expected to get and keep a good enough job to pay the bills. His big responsibility was to support his family.

His wife, then, was supposed to take care of things at home. She cleaned the house, cooked, took care of the children, washed the clothes, and sometimes took care of the yard and garden. For many families, this arrangement worked well because the wife didn't hold an outside job. Homemaking was her full-time job. Anyone who has kept a house clean, cooked three meals each day, and taken care of several small children knows that it is indeed a full-time job.

Marriage Roles Are Changing

Today, however, this picture is changing for two reasons. First, most families can no longer get along on one paycheck. Many couples, including those with small children, find they both need outside jobs in order to pay the bills. The wife may work as many hours away from home as her husband does.

The second reason fewer women are satisfied doing "only" the housework is simply the fact that they don't want to. Not all women

like or are good at cleaning house or cooking. Not all women want
the total responsibility of childcare.

> *I'm a nurse's aide. I'm not crazy about the hours, but I like my
> work. I needed to get out of the house. I personally can't stay in
> the house, cook and clean and take care of the kids all day.*
> (Elaine, married four years ago at 16 to Lloyd, 17)

In some families the woman is expected to wait on her husband.
When a young man from such a family gets married, he may expect
the same kind of service from his wife. If she doesn't think this is
right, they will need to do a lot of talking and working through the
problems that may arise.

> *In Jose's family, his mom does everything. His dad only works,
> eats, and watches TV. But I said I wasn't going to do this all by
> myself. I told Jose, "Either you help me out or you can come
> home to a messy house." I watched my mom, who had a full-
> time job, clean house and take care of the kids while my dad
> would just work, and I didn't like what I saw.*
>
> *We were supposed to be partners, I told him, and we needed to
> do this together. Some of my friends thought this was a little
> harsh. They thought I should clean house and take care of the
> baby, play by the rules. But I don't like it that way.*
>
> *I told him I wasn't the only one that makes the mess around
> here. Finally he started helping me. He knew before we were
> married that we were both going to have to work hard on
> everything together, not just me. Now we make it work.*
>
> *When he wasn't working he would clean the bedroom and take
> care of Janet all day while I was in school. Now he's working,
> but if Janet is sick or if I've had a real bad day, he'll either help
> me with Janet while I pick up the house, or he'll start working on
> the house while I take care of Janet.*
>
> *On Sunday we go grocery shopping together and we wash
> clothes together. Actually, we take turns on that—one Sunday I'll
> watch Janet and he'll go to the laundromat, and I'll do it the next
> week.* (Annie, married at 15 to Jose, 17)

If the young couple must live with his family when they're first
married, as Annie and Jose did, it may be especially hard. Even if the
young couple has talked through these differences before marriage and
come to some agreement, his family may be critical of their "equal"

marriage. Sitting down with his parents and discussing these issues
may be helpful.

Two-Paycheck Marriage Preferred

In the marriage attitudes survey, only one-third of the boys and
one-sixth of the girls thought the husband should be responsible for
earning all the money. Slightly more than half the boys and almost 70
percent of the girls thought both should share this responsibility. A few
said it was the wife's responsibility, and the rest said it didn't matter.

The survey showed 41 percent of the girls and 36 percent of the
boys thought husband and wife should share the task of vacuuming
the house. Somewhat fewer (35 percent and 27 percent) said they
should share the task of mopping the floors.

About half the girls and 43 percent of the boys said both should
prepare meals, while almost two-thirds of the girls and more than half
the boys said both should clean up after meals. About half the girls
and only 29 percent of the boys thought both should wash the car.
Even fewer—29 percent of the girls and 16 percent of the boys—
thought both should mow the lawn.

Women appear to be more interested than men in equal marriage
according to this survey.

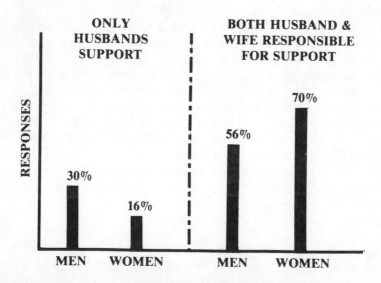

Amy and Kent, married three years ago when each was 19, have learned to share their work:

> Amy: *Roles? We share now. We didn't much before, but now he's helping a lot. I think it was either that or I'd go crazy. You could tell it was too much for me and he knew it was too hard.*
>
> Kent: *I get home first so I do most of my work then when nobody else is in the house. I wash the dishes a couple of nights a week. If her schedule doesn't permit it, mine usually does.*
>
> Amy: *He helps a lot. Just helping with the housework has done a lot for our marriage. I think a lot of women would appreciate that so much—having some of that burden lifted.*
>
> Kent: *If the dishes are done, you can sit for half an hour and we spend that half-hour together.*

While many women don't want to do all the housework and child care, not all men enjoy yard work or car repair. More important, many men don't want the total responsibility of earning the money for the family. The stress of having a wife and children solely dependent on his paycheck can be very difficult.

Shared Roles Work

More and more couples are deciding to share both roles. Each has a paying job and each shares in the housework and childcare. Both the man and the woman can benefit. He isn't burdened with all of the financial responsibilities and she doesn't have to do everything at home. Hopefully she will be able to find a job she will enjoy—just as he wants to like his job. He may enjoy some of the household tasks, too. He almost certainly will find he becomes much closer to his children if he is involved in their care.

Other families do a complete role reversal. She works away from home and he becomes a househusband. If one paycheck is adequate and both partners prefer this approach, wonderful! They are lucky to agree. However, according to the marriage survey, not many teenage women are ready for this plan. Only 10 percent said it would be all right if her husband wanted to stay home while she got a job to support the family. More than three-fourths said it probably or absolutely would *not* be all right.

The reverse was not true. Only 11 percent of the boys said it absolutely or probably would *not* be all right if their wives chose to stay home. Almost three-fourths said it would be OK. True role freedom obviously has not arrived in our society.

But any of these three approaches can work if both partners choose to follow it. Both partners may choose the traditional approach where the husband works and she takes care of their home. (We'll talk about childcare later.) Or she can work while he keeps house. Or both can work and both can share housekeeping tasks.

Two Essentials: Paycheck, Housework

There are two other possible approaches, neither of which works well. If neither partner wants to hold a paying job, trouble looms ahead. Unless they are independently wealthy, they will have obvious problems with no income. Welfare grants do not provide enough money to live as most people want to live.

Perhaps their parents will help out for awhile, but help from parents is likely to run out at some point. Anyway, most young people cherish their independence. If Mom and Dad are paying the bills, they're probably also making many of the decisions.

So most of us would agree that someone needs to earn some money. Both partners can't stay home and keep house. Most of us would also agree that someone needs to wash the dishes and sweep the floors, at least occasionally. So what happens if both partners *choose* to hold outside jobs—or find that both *must* work away from home? What if neither one wants or has time to do the housekeeping chores?

Traditionally, the person holding the job doesn't work at home. Perhaps your father was lucky enough to come home tired after a day's work, and be able to sit down to a hot dinner. After dinner he read or watched TV while your mother cleaned up the kitchen. Your mother probably didn't have a full-time job. If that was their division of tasks, fine.

But that model still exists in many homes in which both partners work at a full-time job. Many husbands still expect their wives to clean the house, cook the meals, and take care of the children in addition to working or going to school full-time.

> *Roles? His basic ideas are to make sure the wife takes care of the house and the kids, does the cooking...even if I'm working. But things have changed a lot—it's not like the olden days when the man made the money and the wife took care of the home.*
> (Glenna, married at 16 to Dennis, 20)

More Women Work Today

This is a particularly difficult situation today because of the rapid change-over from most women staying home to the current pattern of the majority of women working. A generation ago, even if a woman held an outside job, she may have felt it was her duty to take care of the house too. That was the accepted practice.

Today, for many women, this is not the accepted practice. Some men, however, have been raised to believe that women take care of the house and kids. That was what their mothers did, and that is what they expect from their wives. Arlene, married at 18 to Dale, also 18, tried working away from home:

> *I'm in charge of cleaning house all the time. He thinks that if he works, that's enough for him to do. He wanted me to go out and work so I could learn something, so I got a job in a store.*
>
> *I got real mad because he wouldn't help me. I worked 8-5, and he would pick up Chrissie at 4:00. He would have an hour with her. He had said, "When you start working, I'll help you clean up and I'll help you cook." But he didn't. I would come home and the house was all torn up and I had to cook. I tried for a month. But it didn't work, so I quit. I said there is no way I'm going to work, then come home and clean and cook.*

Ed, 18, and Sally, 17, have been married six months. Sally, who is pregnant, is a senior in high school. Ed said:

> *Roles? Pretty traditional. I try to be helpful. I know sometimes I don't do as much as Sally would like. I think I get my values in this area from my parents. Mom pretty much did this and Dad did that.*

If Sally voluntarily did everything at home now, she would be setting a pattern in their marriage that would be hard to break. Instead, she is gently encouraging Ed to become more involved in their home. He's trying. When their baby is born and he sees how very busy Sally will be, he may be willing to be truly involved.

To repeat, if one of you wants to work and one of you wants to stay home, great. You can probably work out a fair and acceptable division of tasks. This works if two things are happening: The person working should be earning enough money to support your family. The person staying home should be the kind of homemaker you both want.

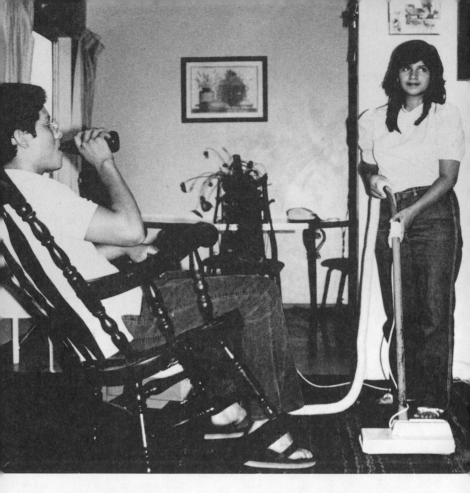

We seem to have pretty traditional roles. I don't have to work, so I'm home right now. Don prefers it this way since Susan was born. Both of us realize the household responsibility would be on my shoulders anyhow. He would just as soon have me home because things work smoother for him with me here. I'll probably have a career later. (Rebecca, married at 21 to Don, 25—her second marriage)

Problem of Housework

But what do you do if both of you must or want to work, but neither wants to get involved in the cooking, cleaning, laundry, and other tasks at home? That's the problem faced by many young (and older) couples today.

First, if you aren't yet married or living together, talk a lot about how each of you feels about the subject. If you're a girl dating a boy who makes cute remarks about "woman's work," don't ignore it. Ask what he means. Think through together how you would handle lots of different situations. What if he's injured and can't work? Or simply can't make enough money to support your family? What if you get sick and can't cook and clean for awhile? What if you decide you want a job?

If either of you thinks one paycheck will be enough, remember that lots of families need two paychecks to pay their bills. Talk about sharing the many tasks necessary in running a pleasant home if both of you are working.

You may already be living with a partner who expects you to do everything at home, yet you have a job or you're going to school. You're holding *two* jobs if you're doing all the homemaking tasks in addition to outside work. If you don't like doing so, you need to change things. Elaine has this problem:

> *Yes, we have traditional roles and it's not easy. I work 11 P.M. to 7 A.M. and it's not OK with me to come home and do all the housework. I was trying to talk to him about it the other day.*
>
> *He won't help in the house at all. I only get five or six hours of sleep each day, then I'm up grocery shopping, paying the bills. I'm not happy with it. I want him to help. He tells me, "I never had to do that at home," which makes me mad.*
>
> *His mom didn't work until he was 14, and when I'm not working, he doesn't do anything either. But when I'm working, I need help. If he sweeps the floor once, he thinks that's his help for the month.*
>
> *I feel they should help. I really do. A marriage is a 50-50 union. When you're working and he's working, I don't think it's fair that he comes home from work and wants his dinner immediately.*

Psychologist Suggests Retraining

Jean Bayard, psychologist, Cupertino, California, talked about couples in this situation. "If your husband was brought up not to do 'woman's work'," she advised, "you have to retrain him. You need to tell him things need to be different. You do everything and he does nothing at home and you don't think it's fair. You can't help it if that's the way he was brought up—that's not the way it's going to be.

"If he thinks it's fair that you should do everything, you have to change his views of what's fair. It will take some real persistence to stick with it. But if you want to live the kind of life you want, you either have to train him to live that way or find someone who will go along with your sense of fairness."

Yvette, 17, and Vince, 19, are slowly hammering out their way of coping with jobs and housework. She said:

> *About three months ago we were fighting a little. He would say, "The house is too dirty," and I would say, "You have to help me if I'm working."*
>
> *Right now I'm taking care of Joey during the day and at night he takes care of him. I get home from work about midnight and go to bed. In the morning I clean up the house and fix dinner for Vince. He comes home about 3:30 P.M. and takes care of Joey. I go to work then. So right now he's helping me and I'm helping him.*
>
> *At first he didn't really like that. He would say, "I'm coming home from work and I'm tired." I would say, "Well, I'm coming from work and I'm tired too."*
>
> *We talked about it. I said if we really want to keep our marriage together, we have to talk. If I don't like something, I need to say, "Vince, I don't like this," and he has to do the same.*

Dr. Bayard discussed the matter of self-image: "Does your man think it is effeminate to sweep the floor or take care of the baby? You may be able to help him understand that it's a strong man who can handle these things well." Jean was tolerant of Dick's feelings on this matter:

Dick helps me clean the house. He won't do the dishes or the bathroom but he will vacuum and clean up. But when he does, he closes the curtains. If his friends come over, he quits—he doesn't want to get caught doing housework! I think he's willing to do it only because when he was home his mom used to make them all do part of the housework. He was used to it. (Jean, married at 16 to Dick, 18)

Shari and Ruben were married soon after she graduated from high school. He had dropped out in eleventh grade. Shari's advice is similar:

I feel the work needs to be 50-50. Even if the woman doesn't work, but is taking care of a child, she's bushed. When you hit that bed, it's like a rock. You're tired! He has to pitch in. In the beginning you start teaching your husband, start having him help you. You don't necessarily tell him, but let him learn on his own.
There are lots of ways to do it. Let him try out the different jobs and let her try them out. See who handles each task better.

Ruben responded to his wife's comments:

It's 50-50 now. I wash dishes, I vacuum, I clean toilets. She works. I used to say, "I'm not going to wash no dishes. I'll throw out the trash, I'll do the yard, but I won't wash no dishes." But she has taught me a lot of things.

Sharing Child Care

Tammy, 17, is also helping Rick, 18, become more involved:

When we lived with my parents, Rick never helped me do dishes or anything else around the house. But as soon as we moved here to our apartment he started helping me with the dishes. That's good because I'm getting Lisa into bed about then.
He still doesn't do much taking care of Lisa. If I'm home he won't change her diaper unless I'm really busy. He never bathes· her. Occasionally I can get him to feed her if I'm lucky.

Tammy works half-time. She's doing her best to help Rick understand that he's ahead if he's truly involved in the care of his daughter.

A lot of us might prefer never to wash a dish or sweep a floor. We know these tasks must be done, so we try to work out a system in which neither partner does all the dirty work.

But parenting is a different matter. When it comes to parenting, to caring for our children, we miss out on a lot if we expect/let the other parent do it all. Many young mothers report that their partners don't "like" to change diapers. Naturally. Who really "likes" to change a diaper?

But diaper-changing has its positive side—and not only because Baby needs a dry diaper. This is a wonderful time to communicate with your baby. If Daddy doesn't do his share of changing, not only is Mother likely to be too busy, but, more important, Daddy is missing out on an enjoyable part of parenting.

> *Derek is involved a lot in Johnny's care. He feeds him and changes him, and he plays with him a lot. He spends a lot of time with him. Sometimes he suggests that I go out and he'll play with him and put him to bed.* (Gloria, married at 18 to Derek, 18)

Have you ever heard a mother say she can't do something because she's "baby-sitting" her own child? Probably not. She's taking care of her child, and that's all. But you've undoubtedly heard a man say, "I can't go tonight because my wife's gone and I have to baby-sit." Actually, he was saying he would be caring for his child that night.

The words we use often reveal our values. Generally we speak of baby-sitting when we're talking about taking care of someone else's child. If Daddy says he's "baby-sitting" his own child, what is he really saying? That his child "belongs" only to Mother?

The vast majority of both boys and girls in the marriage survey thought it was important that both parents play with and discipline their children. Almost all thought it was important for parents to agree on how they discipline their children.

If both parents are expecting to have a good relationship with their children, as these survey results indicate, then both parents need to be deeply involved with those children from the day they're born. In fact, research suggests the family is likely to have a closer relationship if Daddy is there *before* delivery. If he learns the prepared childbirth techniques along with his wife, he can be involved in the birth of his child.

Too often, a father waits for baby to "grow up" before acting as if the baby is truly his child too. Both father and child miss out on a lot if mother does most of the parenting.

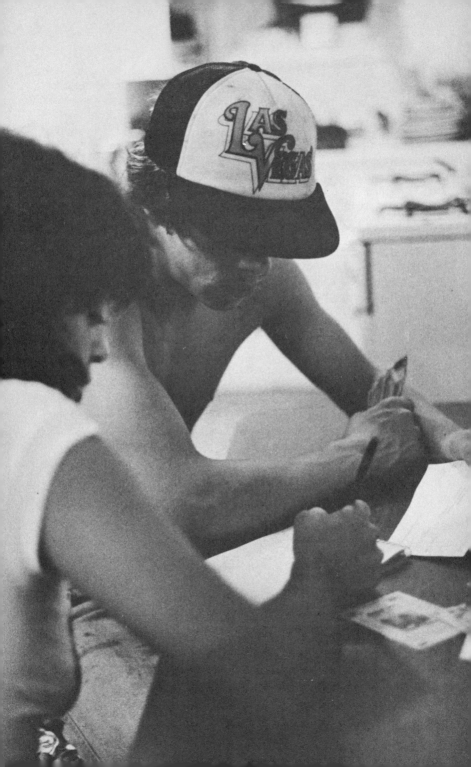

Chapter 7

*God, I wish we had money. Security.
Living in this junky little apartment
gives me lots of stress. I want to get
out of here. If we just had some savings
to fall back on, some security.*

*It's funny how money can cause
little fights. We get into fights
because I get bored staying home.
But if we had money we wouldn't
have to stay home all the time.*

(Melodie, married at 17 to Brett, 19)

The Bills
& Budget Blues

*I'd been working since I was 15, so I thought when Arlynne
and I got married it would be no problem. But later on I got laid
off and it was hard to find another job. We had a little savings to
tide us over, but I'd never been too careful with money. I didn't
have any reason to be because before it was just money for me.
But it takes a lot of managing to make it stretch now.* (Cameron,
married at 17 to Arlynne, 16)

*When he's laid off you still have to pay the rent, the utilities,
and make sure the baby has her food. My mom was a single
parent, and I knew it was hard for her to take care of us. I knew
that getting married doesn't put you on easy street. There are a
lot of responsibilities.* (Arlynne)

Cameron, Arlynne, and Melodie speak for many teenage couples.
Most of the young people we interviewed for this book spoke of
money problems. Almost half the young people in our survey who
were living together and/or married said money—or the lack of
it—has been a greater problem than they expected.

Almost No Income for Some

Most couples who marry while they're still in high school simply
don't have much money. At this stage it may not be so much a
question of how to spend the money or who spends it. It may be more
a question of surviving with almost no income.

If both are under 18 and they have a child, they may qualify for aid
from welfare under the Aid to Families with Dependent Children
(AFDC) program. This, of course, provides a very minimum income.
Or their parents may still be supporting them. If they are, the young
couple may live either with his parents or hers.

Several of the married teens I interviewed talked about the problems
caused by having almost no income. Suzanne's marriage didn't survive
the stress of her husband never working. They were divorced about a
year after the wedding. She said:

*I wanted to keep growing, to go to college. But he didn't want
me to and his parents didn't want me to either. They didn't even
want me to work. I still don't know how they expected us to get
along because he wasn't working—and somebody had to pay the
bills.* (Suzanne, married at 17 to Bill, 19)

Elaine, married at 16 to Lloyd, 17, discussed the money problems she and Lloyd still have even though both are working. She also talked about their early years together:

> *I don't know how we did it. I'm surprised Lloyd and I are still together—we've been through so much. My mom kicked him out several times and he lived in the car. That was hard for me, too.*
>
> *Well, you see, Lloyd wouldn't work. This is the first job he has held this long—and we've been married four years. He likes to play with cars all the time and he finally found a job as a mechanic where he can do just that—play with cars.*
>
> *That makes a big difference because now we know where the money is coming from. Now we don't have to depend on welfare. That always ate my pride up, having to cash those checks. Plus now he's not home all the time. That's another thing that used to get to me. He was constantly home.*
>
> *I never really accepted his not working. We used to fight a lot, argue a lot. His mother even says she doesn't know how I put up with him, that I should have left him long ago. But I think we'll stay together—if we loved each other enough to stick it out this far, we'll continue!*

Lena and Tom, married two years ago at 16 and 18, have similar problems. They don't know how much longer their marriage can last. Tom said:

> *Most of our arguments are because there is no money. Lena needs clothes, the kids need clothes. My parents help as much as possible. Sometimes I find side jobs that help. I have unemployment insurance now.*
>
> *I believe in the traditional roles. I would rather have Lena stay home, but until we have enough money to settle down, she may need to work too. I feel embarrassed not working.*

Lena talked about her understanding and her resentment of Tom's lack of a steady job:

> *It's rough with no money. He doesn't work. We tried welfare but we didn't stay on it. I have this little part-time job here at the apartment that pays the rent. My mother-in-law supplies the food for us. But he's not interested in working, so our fights are always about that.*

He'll get a job and keep it for maybe a month, long enough to keep me quiet. Then he quits. He had a job when we got married, but he quit the next week. He tells me he has an appointment for an interview, then he stays in bed and won't go.

I think he feels insecure. He has gone through three or four jobs. One paid pretty well, but he quit that one too. He says he doesn't like working with his hands. He wants a job where he sits behind a desk. We'd be divorced if it weren't for the kids.

Importance of Job Skills

Both Lena and Tom have finished high school, but neither has much in the way of job skills. If Tom believes in the traditional roles, he apparently is not expecting Lena to support the family. He appears to feel defeated by his many responsibilities as the married father of two children. Lena's comment, "I think he feels insecure," is probably quite accurate.

If Tom could get some career counseling he might become more aware of what he wants to do with his life. If he could pin down a job area which really interests him, maybe he could get some training and eventually have the kind of job he wants—if it's "behind a desk," fine. Whatever he decides to do, Tom needs a great deal of encouragement.

Sometimes taking a class can inspire a person to figure out his/her talents and to look aggressively for a job. Sometimes that isn't enough—a lot of people find it hard to get a good job. But talking to the career counselor at the local junior college would be a good place for Tom to start.

If they can find someone to care for their children, they may decide both Lena and Tom should be working. Of course her problem also is a serious lack of job skills. She, too, should talk to a career counselor.

When Evangelina, 18, and Todd, 21, got married, they talked about whether or not she should work. He said:

Money is our big problem. Evangelina likes to spend it and I like to put it away. She needs to go out and get a job. She'd find out how hard it is to make it. But I'd want her to get something that would pay enough to have someone take care of the kids.

Yes, we follow traditional roles. That was the way I was raised. If she works, it would be the same. My mom did it. She still does. So could Evangelina.

Evangelina doesn't agree:

> *I'd like to get a job but I probably couldn't do it all—work, come*
> *home, clean the house, and take care of the kids. I think it would be*
> *a problem because I would be so tired when I got home.*

Evangelina needs to express her feelings to Todd. It doesn't seem
fair for him to expect her to find a job and at the same time take total
care of their home and children by herself. She can explain that she's
willing to help support their family. If she does, however, he'll need
to share the work at home.

Evangelina is talking about going back to school. She never finished
high school, and she knows the lack of a diploma means she's very
limited in the jobs she could find. "I don't want to cook our meals,
then go out and cook hamburgers all day at minimum wage," she said
wistfully.

Sharing Money Management

Teenagers sometimes become skillful at getting money from their
parents. It's a game they play. If this game continues into marriage,
it's not good at all. A couple needs to put *our* needs, not *my* needs
and *your* needs, at the top of their list.

Sometimes a man feels that if he works while his wife "merely"
keeps house and looks after the children, the money he earns is his to
spend as he pleases. He doesn't think his wife should be involved in
deciding how to spend it. Joni, who was 15 when she married Jeff,
18, had this problem at first:

> *We always argue about money. He thinks because he makes the*
> *money, he has more right to use it. So I say, "No, I clean the*
> *house, I take care of Angela. I'm doing a job too. Just because*
> *you work for the money doesn't mean you earn it just for*
> *yourself." He says it's our money, but he has more right to it.*
>
> *Most of our money goes for payments, and sometimes when*
> *there is a little extra left, I ask, "Can I have a little money?" He*
> *never wants to give me any. I guess he doesn't trust me. Maybe*
> *when I get out of high school I'll get a job so I can have some*
> *spending money.*
>
> *When I want to go somewhere I have to ask him for money.*
> *Last week I went to the Amusement Park with my friends and he*

gave me $3. Everybody else had to pay for most of my rides.
Even his sister told him he should give me some money each
week. But he won't.

Jeff didn't understand why this mattered to Joni:

We do everything together so I just pay for whatever we're
doing. If you go out with your friends, I give you money.

Several months later Joni and I talked again. She described the
changes in their relationship:

He's including me in the financial part now. I clean his mom's
house once a week, and he says, "Now you know how it feels to
work and have your money all gone." Which is true. We work
hard, and then the money is gone for rent, utilities, food.

His mom made us about five envelopes—one for rent, one for
food, another for car expenses, one for utilities, and one with just
a little money for me. It's not much, but now I don't have to ask
Jeff for every cent I need. We get our check, get it cashed, and
we put so much in each envelope. We've tried this before and it
works pretty good if we stick to it.

We've been having to budget lately. I use coupons when I
shop, and I buy store brands. That helps. The day he gets paid
we go shopping together.

Jeff does the bills, the bank statement, everything. I always
thought the lady did all the budgeting, but I don't. Jeff does it
which is fine with me.

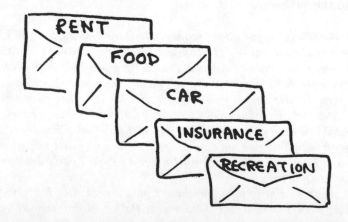

Joni and Jeff are learning some valuable money management lessons. Most important, they're doing their financial planning together now. Their system of budget envelopes is an excellent way of handling fixed expenses before spending money on impulse purchases.

Who Pays the Bills?

Perhaps in your family your mother handled the money while in your partner's family, Dad did. If so, you may have the same problem Tammy, 17, and Rick, 18, had:

> *We're still having problems because he says he's the man of the house and he should carry the checkbook and pay all the bills. But my mother always did this and it makes me feel useless, like I'm just a little child.*
>
> *When we first were married, the checkbook wasn't in my name and I couldn't even write checks. Now I can, but my name should have been on it from the beginning. That would have saved a lot of problems and arguments. I think it's a good idea to talk these things out beforehand because you need to know what to expect. After you're married, it's too late.*
>
> *If you talk about it before you're married you know how the other person will be. It's great if you can agree—but Rick and I never talked about it beforehand. Finances can cause a lot of problems.*

Tammy's right. It's important for a couple to share the money management. To her, not being able to sign checks made her less than a full partner. She and Rick need to talk about their goals and their values, how they want to spend their money *together*.

Do you know how to write checks and balance a checking account? These skills are important when you start housekeeping and paying your own bills.

> *Money is one thing we should have talked about. When we got married I didn't know anything about checking accounts, paying bills, whatever.*
>
> *When we first opened our checking account, we really messed it up. I didn't even know you were supposed to balance your checking account. He had no idea either. We would get these statements and I would just throw them away.*

> *Then three months later our rent check bounced and I couldn't understand it because I knew my math was right. But I hadn't deducted the $4 check charge. When the check bounced, he didn't blame it on me although he did think we were both being a little stupid. So we went to the bank and they explained it all to us.* (Gloria, married at 18 to Derek, also 18)

If you don't know how to balance a checkbook, find out! You can also pay bills with money orders instead of checks if you prefer.

When a Budget Is Necessary

Most people aren't interested in working out a budget until they have money problems. A lot of us go along spending as we want/need to, figuring it will all work out. If we're doing that, we generally aren't even slightly interested in thinking about a spending plan. Not until we see that it isn't working out—that our bills seem overwhelming— are we ready to think about budgets.

For example, one day I was talking with a group of pregnant teenagers about the expenses of raising a child. One young woman said, "I just spend the money until it's gone and then I don't have any for the last week of the month. I'd rather do that instead of budgeting. That would take all the fun out of it."

But when she was asked if it mattered if there was no food for the baby during that last week of the month, she said, "Of course. That's different." She wasn't ready to talk about budgeting right then, but she probably will develop an interest in the subject sometime after she has her baby.

Rosemarie and Steve, both 16 when they married, lived with her parents for a year until she graduated from high school. A few months later they moved into an apartment. Then the real trouble began. Rosemarie said:

> *We lived off our parents for so long, we took it for granted. When we moved out on our own and had to manage our own incomes, we spent a little crazy. Then when the rent came due, we would go to Mom and Dad and say, "We need the money." They helped us once, then said, "Look, you have to do it on your own." The problem was we didn't learn from that. We still spent a lot that we didn't have.*
>
> *I think we got into too expensive an apartment. We bought furniture, thought "Credit is great," and got in over our heads*

*because we had all these charge accounts and had credit
everywhere. So we thought we had more than we did.*

*After Steve and I were divorced, Helen and I lived with my
sister for a year. While I was with her it hit me that I had only
one income to support myself and my daughter. So I planned
what I had to have—basically a roof over our heads and food.
Now that I'm married again, that's how we do it. We plan a
budget every month, pay for the things we have to have. Then, if
there is money left over, we go out to eat.*

*My husband realizes that necessities come first rather than
bringing out the charge card. I've learned in the past couple of
years how to do it. In fact, we have a budget now that we xerox
each month. We follow it pretty carefully.*

Keep Track of Expenses

If you've decided you need to cut back on expenses, where do you
start? You may have some areas where you know you're overspending.
Or you may be thinking, "We can't cut back. We buy only what we
really need."

Whatever your situation, the place to start is *not* to sit down at
once and write out a firm spending plan in which you cut everything
in half. You won't follow it. You'll get upset. And you'd be right.
Some of your expenses can't be changed without a drastic change in
your life style, a change you don't want and may not need to make.

Instead, start your "Let's spend less money" project by keeping
track of everything you spend for at least one week, preferably for a
month. You already know what you'll spend for rent. How much are
your monthly utility bills? Do you have a car payment? Keep track
in detail of car expenses. Don't forget the insurance payment even if
it's not paid every month. What other monthly bills do you have? Do
you pledge a certain amount to your church? Are you paying monthly
doctor bills and/or health insurance? Do you have installment
payments to make?

Add all of these payments up. Your total tells you the specific bills
you must pay each month.

Now comes the hard part. Write down every cent you spend—and
ask your spouse to do the same. Either or both of you may feel this
kind of recordkeeping takes much of the joy out of spending. But
remember, this is a very short-term project.

Perhaps you'll agree to keep track only for one week. A month
would, however, give you a more accurate picture of your
spending pattern.

Each time you eat out, keep track of the amount you spend. Each time you buy a coke or a beer, do the same thing. Perhaps more important, keep track of what you're spending at the supermarket. How much of your money goes for convenience foods such as TV dinners? Does either of you pick up a lot of expensive snacks which add very little to the nutritive value of your meals?

What about clothes? Does one of you feel the other spends "a lot" on clothes? Keeping track of the amount will at least clarify the issue.

What are you spending for recreation? Often, we think it's our spouse who overspends, not ourselves:

> *My husband has extravagant tastes—including this pool table. Would you believe it was set up in this tiny apartment livingroom for six months? Then you see the recorder and stereo over on that wall. He wants a computer. Getting Jimmy to save money instead of spending it on his little toys is hard.*
>
> *It's hard for me because he grew up so poor that now he wants some nice things. We had nice things so I don't have that terrible need to buy.* (Lauri, married to Jimmy when both were 18)

If you have a child, how much do you spend on him/her? Parents often feel their child is "worth" whatever they spend. Of course s/he is "worth" it—but who are you really splurging for when you buy that expensive toy? Your toddler would probably prefer to play with something from your kitchen.

How much are you spending for baby food? Disposable diapers? Keep track.

Be sure you both realize, however, that this brief attempt at writing down everything each of you spends is simply an information-gathering method. At this point, it must not be a value-judgment issue. If you have thought for a long time that your partner overspends on food items, don't grab that first day's spending record as a chance to say, "I told you so." Keep track but don't think about it right now.

Cutting the Costs of Living

Are there any surprises in your spending records? Where do you see extras you could manage to do without? Only you and your partner can answer that question. But knowing exactly where your money goes is an important part of budgeting.

Food, for example. You're lucky if the two of you agree most of the time. When you consider that you each grew up in a different family with different food habits and different food preferences, it's

amazing you agree at all. But whether or not you agree, no one else can tell you where you should cut back on expenses. For some people, buying a high grade of meat is important enough to cut out snack foods. Someone else may realize they can get enough protein from cheaper cuts of meat and from other protein-rich foods. To cut out snacks would take away an important area of pleasure in their lives.

The same kind of thinking applies to convenience foods such as TV dinners and other already-prepared foods. From a strict dollars and cents standpoint, convenience foods generally offer you less food, certainly less nutrition, for your money than do foods made "from scratch." You're not likely to get as much nutrition or satisfaction from a TV dinner as from a freshly cooked meal—and the TV dinner usually costs more.

This is not true of all convenience foods. If you're going to bake a cake, you'd probably spend more on the ingredients to make it all yourself than you would pay for a cake mix. Frozen orange juice is usually cheaper than squeezing oranges yourself.

If both of you are working fulltime and you can afford them, convenience foods may be an important part of your home management plan. All I'm suggesting is that you and your partner analyze *your* life style. Then decide how to spend your money so that you two get as much satisfaction as possible from the money you have.

Making a Budget

Too often people think talking about a budget is talking about ways to be miserable while saving one's money. But budgeting really should be looked at as a way to get *more* fun out of the money you have. Derek and Gloria, who have been married 16 months, described their budget plan:

> Derek: *It's interesting that you should bring up money right now because we wrote out a budget last week and hung it up on the refrigerator. We've tried to write out budgets before but we never really stuck to them. This time we both sat down and figured out all the bills. Then we wrote it out and we're going to follow it this time. We talk it over. I try not to spend money without telling her and she doesn't spend it without telling me.*
>
> Gloria: *He makes the money and I work on the bills. I balance the checkbook and I pay the bills. I like to do it...I guess it makes me feel important. It's not really hard right now because we don't have a car payment or a house payment yet.*

To work out a budget, choose a time when neither of you is overtired. Hopefully you've both had a good day. It would be unwise to start working on a budget when either or both of you is already feeling crabby.

With your spending record in front of you, work out some simple categories—food, shelter, transportation, recreation, medical, and insurance are some starters. What did you spend for each? Does one look a little heavy? Talk about it—and even more important, perhaps—*listen* to what your partner is saying. A budget works only as well as the people involved are willing to work at making it work.

One very important comment: Don't forget a small slush fund or allowance for each of you. It shouldn't be big because your money will stretch further if you plan together how to spend most of it. But a small amount per week should be budgeted for each of you to spend *with no need to account for that spending*. A few people seem to enjoy keeping track of every cent they spend, but most of us don't. Having a few dollars that are mine, that I don't need to discuss with you, can take a little of the pressure off our money situation.

Dick gets an allowance—$10 each week which is enough because he doesn't buy his lunch—I make it. I also put gas in the car.

We used to eat out quite a lot but we don't anymore. It's too expensive. When I was in school I used to go to that deli every day. If I went back now I'd take my lunch.

I didn't know how to manage money when we got married. That was something I had to learn. I've gotten pretty good at grocery shopping. But if I went without a list I'd just buy everything in sight. Every day when I get dinner I write down everything I use up, and then I take that list to the store.

I have always handled the money. It just worked out that way. He was always too tired to go to the bank to cash his check so I would go cash it and buy groceries. He wasn't too hot on writing checks, so I ended up paying the bills. I had had a checking account before and knew how to balance a checkbook. (Jean, married at 16 to Dick, 18)

Jean's shopping list undoubtedly saves them quite a lot of money. Knowing what you need at the store cuts down tremendously on impulse buying. Another trick—don't ever go food shopping when you're hungry. You'll buy a lot more than you would otherwise.

Apparently Jean and Dick have also worked out a good arrangement for handling the money. He didn't want or like to do that sort of thing. She's willing, she's had some experience in money management, and she finds the time to take care of it. Because she handles the money, it's important that Dick have that $10 each week to spend as he wishes.

Yvette shared the way she and Vince talked through their thinking on money management:

I'm working as a waitress. Now we don't fight about the money. We just put both checks together and put them in the bank. Every month we pay the rent with our checks, and with my tips we buy the food.

At first we had some problems with the money. When I wanted more to pay the bills he would say, "I don't have any." But I told him that if we were going to make a good marriage, we had to be together on the money. So I told him if he wanted he could give me his check. We would put it together with mine, and we would pay the bills. Now we even have a savings account for emergencies. (Yvette, married at 17 to Vince, 19)

A big advantage in following a budget is that this so often cuts down on one's impulse buying. Do you know you need to spend this much for rent, that much for food, and more for transportation? If so, it may be easier to say no to the person who rings your doorbell, then tells you about his wonderful photography offer:

> *We've learned not to go for those things that come "something for nothing." We got ripped off on a movie projector and camera. We were supposed to get them free, but they cost us $2000 for lifetime developing. We don't have to develop through that company, but we had to pay for it. So it's paid for, and we're not even using it. But you don't learn these things until it happens to you.*
>
> *People say, "Don't buy anything over the phone. Don't buy anything from people at the door." But until you do it, you don't believe them.* (Elise, married at 18 to Hector, 20)

What About Charge Cards?

Many people talk as if they pay for everything with the "plastic" —their charge cards. This may be convenient, but it can easily lead to overspending.

> *I won't have a charge card. The first year we were married my husband bought me a bed and put it through the finance company. I would rather have spent the money we had instead of going into debt for that bed. Since that time we have made a resolution to pay cash or not buy it. Of course there are a lot of things I'd like to buy on time but you end up paying almost twice as much as what the thing is worth.* (Elise)

It is wise, however, to earn a good credit rating. If an emergency comes up and you have no money, buying on credit may be necessary. But if you have never charged anything, you haven't built up a credit rating. With no credit rating, most stores won't let you buy on credit.

So it's a good idea to charge something you *know* you can afford. Make your payments promptly. This is the way you earn a good credit rating. If you choose not to buy anything else on credit, you're probably smarter than most of us.

> *Our money goes straight to the bank. I pay our bills with checks. We don't have big money problems because I'm not much of a spender. We have credit cards, but I refuse to use them. I don't want to start because before I knew it, we'd probably have bills higher than we could pay.* (Marcella, married eight years ago at 15 to Walt, 19)

Spending Plan Should Suit You

If your money doesn't last from one payday to the next, you have two ways to work at solving the problem. You can try to figure out how to earn more money. Or you can cut back on your spending. Neither method is easy. For most of us, neither method is much fun.

You may be thinking that some day when you have more money, you won't need to do all this budgeting. Certainly having "enough" money to be able to make decisions on how to spend it is a lot better than not having enough to pay your bills. But most people still have money problems even as their income increases. Careful planning always makes that income go further, however.

It's important not to spend more money than you have. It's often wise not to charge a lot of things. It's important to have an emergency fund waiting for that unexpected illness or when your car breaks down.

> *We both want to save money, but it's difficult. Jenny was in the hospital two weeks ago with strep throat and both ears infected. Then Elaine had to go into emergency last week because of her throat. It's things like that. It's always been hospital bills that put us behind.* (Lloyd)

Some people live for the present—and others for the future. Present-oriented people see no reason to save for the emergency that isn't here yet. They prefer to enjoy today rather than sink all their money into a house at some future date.

Future-oriented people are willing to make sacrifices now in order to have a more secure future. Saving for emergencies, planning how to buy a home later are important goals for them.

There are as many different ways to handle money as there are people handling that money. For couples, it's probably most important that they find together a style of money management that fits *them*.

If they are happiest scrimping and saving for that rainy day, that's certainly what they should do. If, on the other hand, both prefer to live more dangerously, they may get away with it. If they don't agree, they need to communicate their different viewpoints to each other. Then they need to find compromises with which both can cope.

To manage money well, the most important thing is for you and your partner to be happy with the way you're managing the money you have. Be sure, however, that *both* of you are involved. It's the agreeing on money matters that's important to your entire relationship with each other.

Chapter 8

> *We lived with my parents, then moved in with his mom. It was hard. We never had any privacy...there was always someone there. We argued a lot and it got on my mother-in-law's nerves. She would start screaming at both of us.*
>
> *Now that we have our own place, it's better. He doesn't walk out like he did when we were there. We can finally talk things out.*

(Jean, married at 16 to Dick, 18)

Moving-In With In-Laws

After we got married we lived at my mom's house for about three months. It felt weird—I wanted to have my own place to take care of. I cooked him his meals, but it just wasn't the same.

It was crowded, but my mom and dad were pretty understanding. They'd go places and leave us alone so we could have time by ourselves. (Pati, married at 17 to Mike, 19)

A little house with a white picket fence used to be the dream of many American newlyweds. A generation ago, this was a reality for lots of young couples.

For many older couples today, even those with good jobs, buying a house seems almost impossible. For many young couples, not only is buying a home not possible, but most of them can't afford to rent an apartment by themselves. An overwhelming majority of married teenagers live with someone else, usually his parents or hers.

Teenagers, as you might expect, say they don't want to live with parents after they're married. Only one in 20 in the survey thought it was a good idea, and about 30 percent said it was "OK until we save some money."

Yet in the survey, 80 percent of those already married and/or living together weren't living by themselves. About one-third lived with her parents, one-third with his parents, 12 percent with other relatives, and 10 percent with friends. Most of the young couples we interviewed were living with or had lived with their parents or other people.

It's Hard to Live with In-Laws

Rowena became pregnant when she and Tom were juniors in high school. They lived with his parents first, then moved to her parents' home:

Even though I was pregnant, my parents told me they didn't want me to move in with him, definitely no. But he wanted me to because he wanted to take the responsibility. He was working and he wanted to support us.

I felt very uncomfortable—it wasn't the same as being home with my parents. It was a different environment. I didn't like living there at all. There were six kids, and all but one were home still. We had our own room, and all I used to do was stay in there and watch TV. I kept all my stuff in that room.

They didn't expect me to do anything. I didn't mind because I didn't feel comfortable cleaning up another person's house. I'd wash dishes, but that was about all. His mom wanted us to move out. I don't know whether she liked me or not, but I think she wanted me to leave. She would tell Tom I was lazy or I didn't know how to take care of little Tommy.

We had no privacy. I kept to myself but I tried to be friendly. Going to school helped a lot. Tom was going to school and working so I didn't see him that much. He worked on weekends too. When I got out of school he'd be going to work—he worked at Burger King until 11 P.M.

I argued with him because I didn't see him as much as I wanted to. His mom used to be always after her kids a lot—it bugged me. Too many kids I guess.

A young man tends to cope a little better living with her parents than his wife does with his. Every situation is different, but the man may be away from the house more than she is. If she has a good relationship with her own parents, she may find it easier to continue living with them rather than adjusting to living with her parents-in-law. If the family can arrange for space for some privacy for the young couple when he comes home, the adjustment should be easier for everyone.

Rowena continued:

Finally we went back to my family and it was a lot better. My dad was working nights so I didn't see him much. We stayed there about six months. Tom was going to night school then. It was just my little sister, Mom and Dad, Tom, little Tommy, and me. There was privacy and it worked out a lot better. Tom felt comfortable there and his parents didn't care.

Then that summer he got a better job working with his dad. That's how we got ourselves together. He works in the warehouse.

Rowena and Tom graduated from high school a few months after their baby was born. About six months later they were able to rent a tiny apartment. They were delighted.

While it may sometimes work better for the young man to move into his parents-in-law's home instead of vice-versa, it's not easy for him either. If he's working hard to support his partner, if he really wants to be responsible for her, he may not feel this is possible in her parents' home.

At first we were living with my parents and that was hard. We were living in one bedroom with everything crammed in there. We

*moved out after a few months. It was hard because Rick wanted
to be the man of the house, yet it wasn't our house and he
couldn't say what goes.* (Tammy, married at 17 to Rick, 18)

If you get married but continue living at home, you may find your
relationship with your parents suffers:

*I had always been close to my parents, but when we got
married and he moved in with us, I got further apart from them.
If something went wrong, I would side with my husband and that
broke down my relationship with my mom.* (Rosemarie, married
at 16 to Steve, 16)

Not Enough Privacy

Over and over these young couples mentioned the lack of privacy.
They could never be by themselves. Most of them had one room they
could call their own—and they spent as much time as possible in
there. Sometimes they didn't even have that.

One young wife I visited showed me some shelves in a closet just
for her things. Her husband had many brothers and sisters and the
house was small. But her parents-in-law had made sure she had a little
space that was entirely hers. She appreciated that.

When a young couple starts living together they need time to adjust
to each other. If they can live by themselves, they may find they more
or less shut out the rest of the world for awhile. They center on each
other. Ideally, this process helps them bond to each other, to become
really close to each other. If they can't have privacy, this may not
happen as easily.

Lauri, now 19, and Jimmy, now 20, have been married three years.
They're renting an apartment, and are finding it very hard to make
the money stretch to cover their expenses. But they agree that having
their own apartment is worth the sacrifice. At first they lived with
Lauri's family. She described that experience, and how they spent as
much time as possible away from the others:

*There were too many people in the house, too many kids. My
oldest sister was there with her three kids, making a total of 11
people living in a small house, and we didn't get along.*

*We hibernated in our bedroom. The only time we went out was
to shower, go to the bathroom, and make dinner. We had a TV
in our room and we didn't associate much with the others. Jimmy
was working, but he wasn't making enough for us to move out.*

Finally my dad got him a better job, and we were able to move in here.

Once we moved out, everybody started getting along. Jimmy holds a few grudges, but you can't solve everything.

"Hibernating" in your bedroom may be the only way you can be alone. Estella, 18, married to Joel, 20, said that wasn't even possible because her husband's little brothers were always coming in to watch TV with them in their room. How can you be alone in a crowded house?

Getting out of the house may be a partial answer. If the weather is nice enough, take walks together. Spending time in a park and finding other places to be alone together may help. If you already have a baby, it gets more complicated. But babies prefer happy parents, and all but the tiniest baby can handle time out of doors with their parents.

Talking over with your family your need for privacy should help. Enlist your parents' help if younger brothers and sisters are forever walking into your room. But first explain your wishes to the brothers and sisters. They might cooperate more than you think.

Some young couples are lucky enough to have a living area they can call their own even if it is part of a parent's home. This was Briann and Victor's situation:

> *They have the den and they're constantly there. The only time Mom is in the kitchen is to cook, and we entertain here in the living room. It's like two different houses.*
>
> *He works Saturday and he gets Tuesday off, so we do what we want in the morning, then we take off all day. On workdays he gets off at 5 P.M. and we usually all have dinner together. Then they go in the den and we watch TV for awhile in our own section.* (Briann, married at 16 to Victor, 16)

Set Up Guidelines First

Living with in-laws is likely to be difficult, especially if the married couple feel their parents are still treating them like children. The parents may, of course, feel they're acting like children. They probably figure if they're old enough to be married, they're old enough to do their share of the work. That "share" may be more for a "grown-up" married son or daughter—even if that son or daughter is only 16. Mother and Dad may have thought their days of taking care of their kids were almost over—and find instead that an extra one has moved in.

Setting up some guidelines before the marriage occurs is important. Many young couples simply don't have the money to set up house-keeping themselves. If they are to live together, it almost has to be with her or his parents. Everyone involved—his parents, her parents, and the young couple—need to be very open about what each wants, what is possible, and how to work out the necessary compromises. It won't be easy!

> *Having two families live in one house was hard, but we made the best of it. We all got along pretty good. My mom had finally let loose—I wasn't her baby anymore. She had her opinions about Kevin, but she knew when to pull back.*
>
> *My dad was traveling a lot so Kevin was like the man of the house and we did a lot of running around for my mom. We stuck together and did what we could.*
>
> *Kevin would help my dad when he was working on something. They'd work together on the cars, and they finally started getting along pretty good.* (Darci, married at 16 to Kevin, 16)

Several positive things were happening here. First, "My mom had finally let loose." Darci's mother realized Darci was no longer her little girl. She started treating her as an adult member of the household.

At the same time, Darci and Kevin were helping with the many tasks of running a home. Kevin won over her father by becoming involved in working with him.

Parents, whether they are yours or your partner's, appreciate it if their adult children take on adult responsibilities. And if you're living with your partner, no matter what your age, you're already playing an adult role. Sometimes the responsibilities that go with that role are hard to handle:

> *Living with in-laws? Don't do it. It's the hardest thing. When I moved in, his dad was going through a separation from his wife. That meant I was the one who cooked and I had to clean the house. His two brothers lived there and I would try to keep the house clean.*
>
> *It caused arguments all the time. We had no privacy. I tell Dale I'll never go back there unless I have to.* (Arlene, married at 18 to Dale, 18)

Who Does the Housework?

Getting the inevitable housework done is a problem in many one-family homes. Put two families together, and it can be a real hassle—another problem mentioned by most of these young people. Annie felt that her mother-in-law imposed on her:

> *We were with his parents for about four months. I had met his stepmother only about a month before we moved in. Those months were terrible. My mother-in-law and I do not get along at all, not at all.*
>
> *For about three of those months I was going to school and she watched Janet during the day. When I came home I usually spent my time with Janet in our room and didn't even bother to talk to Jose's mother. Every night I would do dishes.*
>
> *If Jose didn't come home until late after work, I usually fixed myself a sandwich, but I'd do the dishes anyhow. For about a month that was enough for her, just doing her dishes because she hated doing dishes. She told me she didn't want me to help her with anything else.*

*Then all of a sudden she started complaining because I wasn't
helping her more. She said when I got home from school if the
floor needed sweeping or vacuuming, I should do it. Then she
started leaving and I had to do it all—clean the bathrooms, do
her lunch and breakfast dishes, vacuum—everything but her room
and her kid's room.*

*But she was still telling all of Jose's relatives that I was lazy
and that I didn't do anything, trying to make it look like she did
all the work. So now half of Jose's family doesn't like me but
they don't even know me because of her. And that's really the
reason we don't get along now. If you go over there now, her
house is always a mess. She doesn't have me to clean up
anymore.* (Annie, married at 15 to Jose, 17)

This doesn't sound like a fair division of work. But is it possible
that Jose's mother grew tired of watching Janet while Annie was in
school and Jose was working? Maybe she felt she had taken care of
enough babies without being responsible for this grandchild in
addition to taking care of her house and family.

At first she apparently thought Annie was doing enough if she did
the dishes each night. She thought they would be there only a short
time. But as time went on, and she spent week after week caring for
the baby, she may have decided she needed a lot more help.

The pity in this situation is that they weren't able to discuss their
feelings. Each felt the other was imposing, that she wasn't doing her
share. Jose was caught in the middle. Annie continued her story:

*Jose was angry with his mother because of what she was saying
about me and how she was treating me. But he wouldn't say
anything to her for the same reason I didn't say anything.*

*They got in a few arguments, but that didn't help. We stayed
in a tiny room with a twin bed and the crib. There was a walk-
through space between the bed and the closet—and I stayed in
that room all the time.*

*We stayed longer than we had planned. We'd save the money,
then we'd have to spend it on something else. The second week
we were there, Janet got the croup and we had to rush her to the
hospital. We had X-rays to pay for and the doctor. We had
almost $200 saved up and we had to spend it on that.*

*Jose and I still argued every once in awhile because I wasn't
happy there. Finally we moved into our own apartment. Things
started getting a lot better when we were on our own. I could do
things my way. I could take care of Janet and Jose the way I
wanted to without her telling me what to do.*

Annie and Jose weren't able to move out sooner because they didn't have the money. Savings had to be used for unexpected illnesses. They were stuck at his parents' house far longer than they wanted to be. What might have helped their situation?

Although every family and every individual within each family is different, the following tactics might have improved the situation somewhat: First, the main problem seemed to be between Annie and her mother-in-law. However, several other people also lived in that house. Would a family conference have helped? Here is a family whose son has returned home with a wife they barely know and a tiny daughter. What changes did they have to make in their life style to make room for them? How could these changes have been effected without so much unhappiness for Annie? And for her mother-in-law?

Working out a schedule of household tasks might help. Annie and Jose needed to remind themselves often that they were guests, that Jose's family had made room for them when they needed a place to live. Was there any way Annie and Janet could be away from the house more often? That, too, might help.

It takes a lot of effort to make a marriage relationship work successfully. It usually takes even more effort to create and keep a good relationship with parents-in-law, especially if you're living with them. But if you love your spouse, the extra effort you spend developing a good relationship with his/her parents will be worth it.

Elaine and Lloyd lived with her mother, but Lloyd had at least as much trouble coping with his mother-in-law as Annie did with hers. While there are bound to be misunderstandings among people who live together, the situation can be especially upsetting if the person in the middle is asked to choose between her/his spouse and parents:

> *It was difficult. We used to fight like cats and dogs. Lloyd and my mom never have gotten along anyhow. They would fight and they would get me mixed up in it. That was even more difficult. They wanted me to choose between them.*
>
> *I had to keep reminding them that I loved them both and I wasn't going to take sides. That's hard, especially when you're newly married and you want to do everything for your husband. But we had to live with my mother, and I kept playing the peacemaker role. It was hard.* (Elaine, married at 16 to Lloyd, 17)

Different Backgrounds Cause Problems

If a couple has widely different family backgrounds, it will take even more care to make the marriage work. If the two families don't speak the same language, it can be especially difficult.

Paul's family speaks mostly Spanish while Alison speaks only English. Although Paul and Alison moved into a small house by themselves, his mother soon moved into a trailer in their back yard. Alison remembers:

> *I hated it because Paul was always over there with his mother, spending time watching TV with his mom—and I would be in the house with the baby. She only speaks Spanish and I couldn't speak much at all. I'd have to ask him what she said and that would drive him crazy.*
>
> *It got to be one big house because they built carports—like a hallway to his mom's trailer. They even made a kitchen for her.*
>
> *I appreciated all the help, but I was lonely all the time. I didn't even iron, she did that. All I did was keep the house clean. She cooked for everybody, washed and ironed. It was like a big happy family but I wasn't quite in it—it was like I was standing on the outside watching.* (Alison, married at 15 to Paul, 20)

Darla and Manuel's Situation

Extended family ties are more important in some cultures than in others. Manuel's family was very close-knit as many Hispanic families are. His sister and her children were living with him when Darla, 16, moved in. She found it hard to cope:

I was about three months pregnant when I moved in with him. He has a house but his sister and her kids (14, 12 and 3) were living with us. Her boyfriend would also come around and move in for a couple of months every once in awhile.

She didn't want to move out. When I first moved in with Manuel, I told him two women can't get along in one house. He said, "Yes, you can. You can take turns cooking and cleaning." But I told him it wouldn't work. He didn't believe me.

I wasn't happy there. I wouldn't rearrange the livingroom. About all I did was stay in the room we slept in. I would clean that room and change things around. As time went on, and I was still pregnant, I told him I wanted the baby to have his own room. I wanted to make a baby's room with playthings on the wall and stuff. But we couldn't do that because the baby was in our room and I had my things up and Manuel's things up.

She kept saying she would move, but she didn't. When the baby came, I was set off, and I wanted to go home and just be by myself and be a family, but we couldn't do that. As time went on, I kept telling Manuel I couldn't hold on any longer. But he would tell me to hold on, that she would move.

I waited and waited and finally got tired of it. I couldn't stand his sister—she believed in jumping to whatever the man wants: "Bring me a glass of water." "Change the TV." I don't see it that way. He has two feet and two hands and there are some things you can do for him, but not to change the TV! He could get up and change it himself but she didn't approve of that.

We had less privacy—that bothered me a lot. We couldn't do what we wanted because they were always there. There were times when we wanted to be by ourselves. Our only privacy was our bedroom. All three of us would be in there. We would be talking and stuff and then the baby would be crying. That would mean she wanted to be out and crawl around. I wanted to open the doors and let her explore, but I couldn't because his sister was there. I couldn't let her crawl in his sister's things.

Manuel was paying the rent—he was buying the house and his sister was paying the utilities. We each bought our own groceries.

*When Manuel would come home I wanted to start cooking and
have the house clean. But she would be there and her boyfriend
would come over and she would start cooking. During those 18
months we probably had about four meals with them. I didn't
feel comfortable with her.*

*So I moved back to my mother's about a month ago. Manuel
and I still talk, but I just want to be myself. I hope he's still
around when I decide to go back. I always wanted us to be a
family, and I always told him I wanted it to last. But it got too
hard for me, too much pressure and I couldn't stand it.*

Manuel added:

*Living with in-laws—that was hard for Darla and me. I guess
you have to make a decision to move or something. It bothered
me too. They got in my way a lot of times. But it's hard to push
out relatives—it's hard. I couldn't make a decision either way.*

*Of course if you've got no heart, you're going to do it—but she
is my blood sister.*

Moving In With Friends

But young couples don't always move in with parents or other
relatives. If they can't afford their own place, they may decide to split
expenses with another young family. LeAnne, 17, and Colin, 19,
moved in with close friends:

*We hadn't really planned on moving out together. But I got
pregnant and I told him I wanted to be out on our own before
the baby was born. So we moved in with another couple because
we thought that would make things easier. We were real good
friends and that worked OK for about a year.*

*They had two kids, both older than our baby, and there were
things I didn't like that she let the kids get away with. Dishes and
the housecleaning were a problem. I felt like I was doing them all
the time and she felt she was doing it all. We sat down and made
out schedules but that didn't work either. Something would come
up and I couldn't do something or she couldn't do something.*

*I didn't know how to cook so she said she would cook and I'd
do the dishes. But she didn't cook half the time and I didn't do
the dishes half the time.*

Of course Colin was on my side and I'm sure Robert was on her side, but they never said anything. It was just me and Lorraine that couldn't get along. We finally moved out.

Whether a young couple lives with his parents, her parents, other relatives, or friends, they are likely to have a difficult time. Lack of privacy, disagreement over who does the housework and how to raise the children are just a few of the problems to be expected.

If you and your spouse can't afford a place of your own, you need to sit down with your families and talk about the best solution to your where-do-we-live question. Once a decision is made, everyone involved will need to work hard to make things as comfortable as possible for everybody.

You and your spouse will also want to plan and work toward a place of your own. If either of you hasn't yet finished school, however, be sure you do whatever is necessary to get those diplomas. If that means accepting help from parents, that's what you need to do.

While a place of your own may not be a practical goal today, it's worth sacrificing now to be able to live as you and your partner want to live later on.

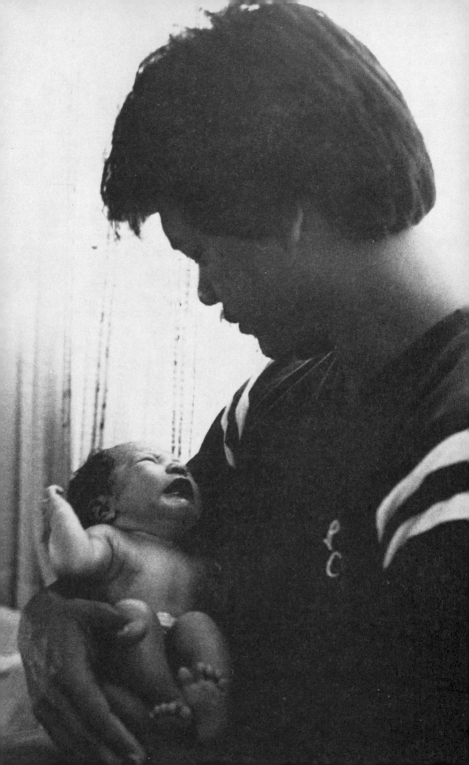

Chapter 9

When Janet was born, our whole life changed. We had gone wherever whenever we wanted. Now we have to think about Janet. We take her with us some places, but we have to plan ahead. We went to the beach last week and it took two hours to get ready! We couldn't stay long because she can't stand much sun.

(Annie, married at 15 to Jose, 17)

Child-Created Commotion

*We love Johnnie, and we wouldn't give him up for the world.
But we had no idea how much time he would take, how much he
would cost. When I was pregnant, I never thought about him
being sick or fussy. It's harder than I thought.* (Gloria, married
at 18 to Derek, 18)

A child creates lots of commotion. There's no doubt about it. Having
a baby changes a couple's lifestyle. Even if their baby is good—
which to most people means a relaxed infant who sleeps a lot—the
parents are going to be very busy. If they have a fussy baby, they'll
wonder if they ever again will get a good night's sleep.

An infant takes lots of time, but generally she'll sleep many hours
each day and, hopefully, each night. As your infant develops into a
toddler, she'll make even greater changes in your lives.

For a more detailed description of life with small children, see
Teens Parenting: The Challenge of Babies and Toddlers by Jeanne
Lindsay (1981: Morning Glory Press). Based on interviews with 61
school-age mothers, *Teens Parenting* thoroughly covers the many
aspects of baby and child care. Emphasis of the book is on the special
needs of very young parents.

Changes Start With Pregnancy

A pregnancy, especially if it's unplanned, may be hard on a
couple's relationship. She may not feel well. Morning sickness affects
some women during the first three months of pregnancy, and for a
few, throughout the pregnancy. Others feel fine physically.

Nearly all pregnant women experience mood swings. Even if she
wanted to get pregnant and she's delighted about the coming baby,
she will have periods of depression. This is caused to a great extent by
hormonal changes occurring in her body because of the pregnancy.
She may cry for no reason. At other times she may snap at her
partner and he'll wonder what got into her.

If the father can be involved in the visits to the doctor and in
reading about the changes brought about by pregnancy, he'll find it
easier to understand these mood swings. *Teenage Pregnancy: A New
Beginning* by Linda Barr and Catherine Monserrat (1978: New
Futures, Inc.) is an excellent resource on prenatal care.

If they can attend prepared childbirth classes together and if he can
coach her during labor and delivery, the baby will seem more "ours"
than "hers."

Darla, 16, described some of the changes Manuel made while she was pregnant:

> *When I first moved in, I was pregnant and he was going out with his friends. Or he would party in the front yard with them, and this was every night. I told him, "The baby is going to come and I won't be able to spend as much time with you."*
>
> *When I was about seven months pregnant, I told him, "Look, the baby is going to come. We have to make some changes." He finally realized what I was talking about. There were times when we spent the weekends by ourselves. His friends stopped coming around for awhile.*
>
> *But then they started coming back when I had the baby. I was in bed with the baby and they were outside partying. I told him we had to change because of the baby. I was tired. As time went on, he started making some time for us.*

About a year later, however, Darla moved back with her mother. She and Manuel are still trying to work out their relationship.

Marriage Relationship Is Primary

New parents are generally astonished at how much time it takes to care for a baby. Sure, some new babies sleep a lot. But some don't. And even when he's sleeping, someone has to do the laundry, prepare his formula (unless he's breastfed), and complete a seemingly endless series of other tasks.

> *She limits the time I can spend with my husband. Leesa is up until 11 P.M. most nights, but Bob goes to bed about 10:00. So all the time he's home I'm doing dishes, fixing bottles, or taking care of Leesa. The little bit of free time I have for myself is usually when he's in the shower.* (Rosemarie, married at 20 to Bob, 24—her second marriage)

Maybe Rosemarie should try Amy's method: "When you have kids, you have to take showers together so you have time to talk!"

Taking showers together is a good idea, but you and your partner need other times alone together without your child. It's important to remember always that, even though you have a child, your relationship with your spouse is still your primary relationship. Eighteen years

of being responsible for a child is a long time. But if your marriage is
forever, you'll have a lot of years left after your children are gone.

> *I think you have to work on your marriage because the kids
> will grow up and move away and you'll still have your husband
> or wife. I think a lot of people get married and have kids, then
> put their whole focus on their kids. They kind of lose touch with
> each other. You need to go out by yourselves, spend some time
> without the kids.* (Pati, married at 17 to Mike, 18)

Is Education Still Important?

One change for teenagers too often brought about by pregnancy is
dropping out of school. About three-fourths of all pregnant
adolescents never finish high school. Many drop out during pregnancy,
while others can't come back after delivery because there is no one
else to take care of the baby.

Yvette almost dropped out, even though she had only a few months
to go to graduation:

> *We were married in December when I was about three months
> pregnant. My husband said he didn't want me to say later, "It's
> because of you that I didn't go back to school." And my school
> counselor said, "I don't want you to blame that kid because you
> didn't graduate."*
>
> *I was tired and it was hard—but I enrolled in the Teen Mother
> Program, managed to get there most of the time, and graduated
> in June. I'm glad I finished.* (Yvette, married at 17 to Vince, 19)

A lot of teenage fathers drop out of school too. It's hard to
shoulder the responsibilities of fatherhood while you're still in high
school—but it can be done, especially if you accept a little help from
other people. If you both graduate, you'll have a better chance at
providing the life you want for your child—and for yourselves.

Satisfying Three People's Needs

If you're married or living with a partner, you know how much
adjusting it takes to learn to live with another person. You each have
needs, and it's hard to satisfy each other's needs often enough.

If you add a baby to your relationship, the changes multiply. While your spouse probably makes at least some effort to please you, to satisfy your needs, your baby will do no such thing. A baby's needs are for satisfying NOW—with no regard for how you're feeling.

> *After Lisa was born it was a lot harder. Rick expected me to do a lot more. Even now he asks, "Well, what did you do all day?" He thinks taking care of a baby takes just a little bit of time. He couldn't understand why I didn't get much done during the day. There are lots of days when she isn't in a good mood and won't play with her toys. He thinks every day should be the same.* (Tammy, married at 17 to Rick, 18)

Most childcare experts today tell us we can't spoil a baby during the first few months after birth. If a tiny baby is hungry, she is in actual physical pain. She needs to be fed at once. If you're sure she's not hungry and you know she's dry, but she continues crying, she probably is lonely. Leaving her to cry it out in her crib is not the way to go. Comfort her and love her.

Of course no one can keep a baby satisfied all the time. If you expect that of yourself, you're doomed to disappointment—and to feeling extremely tired. But you and your baby's other parent will want to do your best to give your baby what she needs—which includes lots of loving.

Think about what that goal means. During the first weeks it may mean feeding the baby every couple of hours. By the time you've changed his diaper, burped him, and rocked him in addition to the feeding, you've spent an hour. You'll feel as though you're spending all your time with the baby—and you may be right.

What do you think this might do to your relationship with your spouse? Maybe you and your partner have been spending most of your spare time together. In the survey of teenage attitudes toward marriage, a majority of the respondents thought it was very important for a married person to spend most of her/his spare time with her/his spouse. In a good relationship, we usually want to spend lots of time together.

A baby's birth can change all that—especially if the couple decides that one person, usually the mother, should take care of the baby.

If Mother is spending most of her time with the baby and she's too exhausted to do anything at all the rest of the time, Father may feel left out. Much is written about the jealous feelings a father may experience as he watches his wife taking care of their baby. Some writers suggest that Mother needs to be sure to give her husband the attention he needs, too, right along with the baby.

This attitude seems unfair to both parents—and to the baby. First of all, Mother already has too much to do in taking care of the baby. She doesn't need the additional job of playing caregiver to her husband. Second, a grown man is likely to feel a little guilty about these very real jealous feelings. After all, he shouldn't feel this way toward a tiny helpless infant. And the baby will be no better off and, in fact, may receive less nurturing as Mother worries about Dad.

Father Is Full Parent Too

There is a solution. The immediate goal seems to be to bring the two parents closer together amidst all the chaos of having a new baby in the house. The other very important goal is for the baby to have as much love, as much chance of bonding with both parents as possible. Bonding means the very special tie that develops between a baby and his mother and, hopefully, father. It depends on lots of closeness between the baby and each parent.

The solution is to include Dad in caring for the baby. Even if Mother is breastfeeding, Dad, when he's home, can still share in all the other care of the baby—the rocking, the burping, the diaper-changing, the daily bath. Incidentally, there is no reason a baby needs a bath in the morning instead of in the evening. The best time is when both parents can either share in this undertaking or take turns. Baby's bath is a very special time for Mother and Dad.

The traditional role-playing of Mother taking care of the baby while Daddy works is certainly not the way to go for many young families today. In fact, it's amazing that childcare is ever assumed to be "woman's work." If parenting is a positive experience (and we must think it is or so many of us wouldn't continue having babies), then both parents deserve to share the joys involved. If it's a lot of hard work (we all know it is), certainly both parents should share that burden.

Most people still think it's preferable for children to have two parents. When both parents are in the home, it's a little silly for that child to see one of them for only a few minutes of play each day. Baby wants and needs real involvement with both parents.

We aren't at all traditional. Sometimes he gets up with Penny at night. When he comes home from work he usually takes over and plays with her, gives her her bath, puts her to bed.

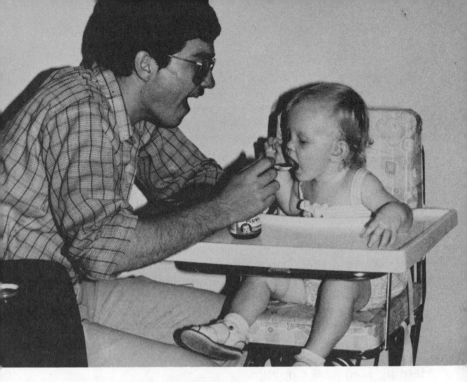

I've seen a lot of families where it usually is the mom that does everything. So I was surprised that Colin helps as much as he does. I never said much. He was right there with her. (LeAnne, married at 17 to Colin, 20)

Seven questions on the marriage attitudes survey dealt with whether the husband or wife "should" do certain things with/for their children. The seven tasks were "Playing with the children," "Feeding babies and children," "Changing baby's diapers," "Disciplining children," "Bathing baby," "Putting baby to bed," and "Putting toddler to bed." Respondents were asked who should perform each task—husband, wife, both, or "It doesn't matter."

A majority of girls and boys, with one exception, answered "Both" to all the questions. Only exception was that only 48 percent (almost half) of the boys thought both should bathe the baby. Almost as many thought the mother should do the bathing.

Ten to 20 percent more girls than boys thought each task should be shared by both parents. Widest difference between boys and girls dealt with "Changing baby's diapers." While three-fourths of the girls said this should be shared by both parents, only half the boys agreed. Many more boys (38 percent) than girls (14 percent) considered this the mother's job.

Many teenagers don't discuss these things before they have sex.
Who is going to say, at a very romantic moment, "Tell me, how do
you feel about changing a baby's diaper?" Or "Do you agree that
fathers as well as mothers should bathe babies?"

If you're pregnant, you may hear the baby's father saying, "No
way will I help with the baby. That's your job. I'll teach him to play
football later." What do you do then?

Parenting involves a lot more than making babies. Some men get
excited at the idea of being a father, but don't want to be actively
involved in parenting. They don't support their partners or their
babies. They don't help with childcare. Planting the sperm, they seem
to think, is doing their share.

A lot of men, of course, work hard at becoming caring, responsible
fathers. You may have a partner who is working hard to support you.
He may have wanted a baby. If he didn't, he figures if you're
pregnant or you already have a child, he'll handle the situation as best
he can.

Helping Dad Feel Capable

OK, so he's supporting you. But you're hoping he will also share
the parenting. You're concerned for two reasons. First, in the beginning
you'll be very tired and you'll need help. Second, and perhaps more
important, he'll be closer to his baby if he's involved. What can you
do to encourage him?

First, make sure he knows you welcome his active involvement in the
care of this baby. *Start as soon after the baby is born as possible.* If
he coaches you through labor and is there with you when your baby is
born, he'll have a good start in fathering. Some hospitals let the
father stay in the room with the mother and baby as much as he
wishes throughout their hospital stay.

> *I think it helped our marriage a lot when he went into the labor
> and delivery room. He told me that watching me go through all
> that made a big difference. He thinks that I did a lot, and he's
> glad to help out with Penny. I know two of my friends didn't
> have their boyfriends go with them and they've both split up
> now.* (LeAnne)

If Dad says he doesn't know how to hold a tiny baby, show him.
Be reassuring. If he insists he can't diaper a baby, help him learn.

Sometimes mothers say proudly, "The baby cries when I hand him to his father. He'd rather I hold him." Think a minute. Would you spend much time holding him if somebody commented on how much he cries with you? Or you can be critical without saying a word. If you adjust the diaper Dad has just put on Baby, you'll reinforce his lack of confidence in his diapering abilities. He may then decide changing diapers is your job.

Give Dad and Baby plenty of chances to become comfortable with each other. You'll all be ahead.

Good Parenting Takes Learning

Most of us aren't born to be "good" parents. It may be natural to love one's baby, but knowing what that baby needs as he develops is not automatic.

Even if you have helped care for little brothers and sisters, you'd be wise to learn as much as possible about babies before yours is born. If you can learn together as a couple, you'll have fewer disagreements later over different approaches to childrearing. If only one of you can take a childcare class, that one should share as much of the class discussions as possible with her/his partner.

Hopefully, Mother and Dad agree on such basic things as nutrition, discipline, and the importance of routines in a child's life. If so, they will find caring for their child is a far easier task. If they argue over these matters, their child will learn to play one parent against the other. In this game, nobody wins.

> Tom wants the kids brought up where you're strict with them. You don't let them drop anything on the floor. They can't mess up anything. But I like to let kids be free, let them mess around and get dirty. He doesn't want Lennie to get dirty. I always thought little boys and girls were supposed to get dirty. (Lena, married at 16 to Tom, 18)

Children need freedom *and* discipline. If Tom and Lena could take a good parenting class together, the discussions there might help them. Tom might learn how important it is for little kids to have times and places to play freely. Lena, on the other hand, might learn more about discipline as teaching, not punishing. She and Tom may need to develop together a consistent pattern of discipline for their children as well as allowing them the freedom they need.

Studying about children together will help you and your partner understand your children's needs. Talk to each other about your opinions and your feelings concerning childcare. If you don't agree, some compromise should be possible.

Grandparents Get in the Act

Sometimes parents agree with each other on childrearing methods, but don't like the way their child's grandparents treat him. If the young family is living with Grandma and Grandpa, this will be especially hard to deal with.

> *You know what's hard? Having two mothers in the house. Kevin's mother believes in spanking the kids all the time and I can't do that. I don't spank my kids. Living with my mom wasn't perfect but she let me raise my kids the way I wanted to.* (Darci, married at 16 to Kevin, 16)

If you live in your parents' home, in some ways you're still under their control. Yet you also know you need to be in charge of your own baby. How do you handle the disagreements over childcare?

First, be sure you're doing a good job of caring for your baby. Be as informed as possible about childcare in general and especially about your own baby's needs.

Then, if your parents disagree with what you're doing, talk about your reasons for thinking as you do. Explain why you think you can't spoil a tiny baby, for example. Tell them why you want to satisfy her needs as completely as possible during these early months. If you and your spouse are in agreement, your parents may be more interested in your viewpoints.

Remember, too, that your parents have had experience in caring for at least one baby—you—and the results are pretty good! Their experience may be very helpful to you and your spouse as you get acquainted with your new baby and his needs.

What About Money?

Most couples find their money problems get worse when they have a child. First, if you don't have good medical insurance, the expense of having a normal delivery is amazingly high.

If a Cesarean delivery is required or other complications develop, costs zoom much higher.

If the baby is bottle-fed, you'll find that formula is quite expensive. Economy is one reason you may want to consider breastfeeding. The other major immediate expense is a supply of diapers. Many young parents are using disposable diapers for about the same reasons that most of us prefer Kleenix over a cloth handkerchief. They do save some work. They're a wonderful luxury.

But that's what they are—a luxury. If you can afford paper diapers, great. But realize what you're doing. Just because "everybody" uses them doesn't mean you have to, too. Take the time to figure the cost per year in using cloth diapers versus diaper service versus disposable diapers. When you're figuring the cost of using cloth diapers, know that you will need about four dozen, and include the cost of laundering them in your cost comparison.

You may be told by a diaper service salesperson that their service is actually cheaper than buying and washing your own diapers. Ads for disposables will suggest they are cheaper. But if you read the fine print—or ask the salesperson some questions—you'll find they're counting the market value of your time in their comparison.

They include the detergent and laundromat expense in washing diapers. In addition, they count the amount you would be paid if you

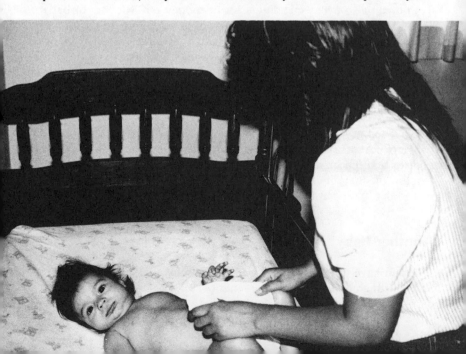

were working at a good job during the hours you spend washing, drying, and folding diapers. For most of us, that's not a valid comparison.

Diapers can be folded while you watch TV. You wouldn't be earning money doing something else if you weren't folding diapers. So it really doesn't make sense to include that in your cost comparison.

If you do your comparative shopping carefully, you'll find that paper diapers cost at least $350 to $500 *more* per year than would buying cloth diapers and washing them yourself. Cost of the diaper service lies somewhere in between. The difference can be even more if you buy the highly advertised and most expensive brands of paper diapers.

> *I won't use paper diapers except when we're on vacation. I think it's crazy to spend all that money on throw-aways. It's not that big a deal to wash and fold diapers. Besides, I think Janet likes cloth diapers better.* (Annie)

You and your partner may decide there are other luxuries on which you'd rather spend that $350. Your baby won't care. In fact, some babies are allergic to paper diapers. Because the more expensive brands are more likely to be highly perfumed, it's these brands that tend to cause allergies in some babies.

You can also avoid spending a lot of money on little jars of baby food. We know now that it's best to wait at least four to six months after birth before giving a baby any solid food at all. Most babies do best on formula or breast milk alone during this time.

By nine or ten months, your baby probably will be eating chopped and mashed (but nonseasoned) food from your table. Instead of buying strained food for those few months between, you may prefer to make your own. You can do so very easily either with a blender or a babyfood grinder. The latter can be bought for very little money.

Many parents spend money on elaborate toys for their baby. Before you do that, check a good childcare book for suggestions. Many of the toys on the market aren't especially effective as playthings for an infant or toddler. You can find better "toys" in your kitchen cupboard.

Another Baby? When?

If you have one child, how soon, if ever, do you want another? Some young couples who got pregnant the first time because they didn't use birth control still don't bother with contraceptives after their baby is born. Needless to say, this is not wise unless you want a second child right away. Tammy and Rick agreed to wait:

> *How many children? Perhaps a total of four. But I'm going to wait about three years between this one and the next so I can get Lisa out of diapers and more independent.*
>
> *She took a lot of time when she was a baby, but now that she's starting to walk, she takes even more time. She's into everything! I think if I had another baby right away I'd not be able to give her the time she needs.*

Arlene and Dale aren't sure they'll have any more children. Their daughter is three:

> *My mom says, "When are you going to have another child, Arlene?" I tell her I will if she'll have it for me. I'm still young and I want to enjoy life and I want Chrissie to have what she needs. If we had another baby, we couldn't do that.*
>
> *Sometimes now we'll go off for a weekend by ourselves. Last month we took off for a concert—three days without Chrissie. We missed her, but it was real nice. Usually my mom will watch her for the weekend because she understands. "You guys, you got to get away." Sometimes I'll go over there and say, "Mom, this kid is driving me nuts." She'll say, "You guys need a vacation. Plan something and I'll watch her." She's real good about that.*

If you don't want another baby immediately after the first one, using a contraceptive each time you have sex is absolutely necessary. Breastfeeding doesn't prevent pregnancy. You can get pregnant very soon after delivering a baby. Ask your doctor to help you choose the best birth control method for you and/or your spouse.

It's possible to have a good marriage without children. Many people, however, consider children an important part of their future plans.

Children are expensive. They take an awful lot of work. Their parents are responsible for them for 18 long years. In return, they often give a great deal of pleasure to their families.

As you and your partner make plans for your future together, you may decide to include children. If so, be prepared for great changes in your lives. After you have a baby, nothing is ever the same again.

Chapter 10

> *We're both real jealous. He looks at other girls and I ask him, "What are you looking at?" He thinks he sees other guys looking at me, at what I'm wearing. We talk about it. When we first got together, when he got mad, he wouldn't talk to me. We were always fighting, but later we got real open with each other. That helps.*

(Estella, married at 17 to Joel, 18)

Jealousy... Green-Eyed Monster

> *Jealousy used to be a real bad problem with both of us. It was like I couldn't go anywhere and neither could Colin without a hundred questions being asked—"Did you pick up?" That kind of thing. I always thought it was all right for me to talk with a boy and know it was just a friendship relationship and that was it. But he didn't know that. And if he was to talk to a girl, I wouldn't know that.*
>
> *So about a year ago I told him, "You can have girlfriends and I want to have guyfriends."*
>
> *He said, "Well, if that's how you want our relationship to be."*
>
> *I said, "Why, we've got to have friends of both sexes." We're very open and I tell him everything. I think that helps keep the jealousy down.* (LeAnne, married at 17 to Colin, 20)

Jealousy isn't even listed in the index of most marriage books. But many teenagers (and older people) find their jealous, possessive, and anxious feelings cause them and their partners a lot of misery. An amazing number of arguments start with jealousy.

Elise and Hector have been married five years. They still have trouble with jealousy:

> *We're both jealous on and off. Sometimes he is if I dress up to go to work, like today. I usually wear pants, but if I dress out of the ordinary, he's jealous. And sometimes I'm jealous when he dresses up nice to go out with the guys.*
>
> *He knows pretty much that I'll stay home, that I won't go out looking for something else. But I still have my doubts with him because he goes out with his friends so much. There will always be that doubt until he stays home most of the time.*
>
> *I've caught myself jumping on him as he comes in the door—"Where have you been? What have you been doing?" And there is no reason—except I have these doubts inside.*

Marriage Survey Indicates Jealousy

More than half of the 608 boys in the marriage attitudes survey said they would be jealous if their girlfriend or wife "looked at other boys." About one-third said they would be jealous if she talked with other guys. One in four would be jealous if his partner worked with boys. Almost as many indicated a problem if she went to school with boys.

Almost three in four don't want their partner to go to a concert with another boy, while slightly more than half said they would feel jealous if she had a close male friend.

Darla moved in with Manuel when she was 16 and he was 19. She moved back home a year later. He had hit her several times, mostly because of his jealousy. Darla said:

> *When Manuel hit me this last time I said he had no reason to do that. He said, "Don't you know a man is jealous of his girl?" I told him he never said that before and he said he lied.*
>
> *I used to show my jealousy a lot and he would get his kicks from it. "Man, she's real jealous." So I shined it on and didn't show it.*

Then Manuel explained his feelings about jealousy:

> *I really ain't jealous—but the mind is dirty and you don't know what's going on out there. You know men and you know how they are and you don't trust them. If you're not jealous at first, you'll turn jealous.*

About the same percentage of girls as boys would be concerned if their boyfriend or husband looked at other girls or talked with other girls. Fewer, however, would worry if he worked or went to school with other girls.

Girls responded with more jealousy to the idea of their partner taking another girl to a concert. They were less jealous than the boys with the thought of their partner having a close friend of the opposite sex.

Annie and Jose have been married a year. They had moved to another state, but Annie was back home for a visit. She said:

> *Jealousy? He still has a terrible problem with it. He was going to buy me a new wardrobe last month. But when we decided I would come out here, he said, "We'll wait until you get back." He didn't want me to have any new clothes in case I ran into old boyfriends here.*
>
> *That's one thing we need to work on. It's all in his head. I have never given him a reason not to trust. We need to work on that. I have a friend who has been a good friend since I was in kindergarten, a boy, and Jose doesn't understand that. He used to have a good friend who is a girl, and I don't mind. I won't give up my friend just because Jose is jealous.*

Reasons for Jealousy

Why do so many of us have these jealous feelings? If we think about it, even going to a concert with another friend might make sense. I might not enjoy the same type of music my partner does. Or I might not be able to go on that particular night. If he has a friend who happens to be a woman, why should I feel threatened if she keeps him company?

While our heads may tell us it's OK, many of us wouldn't cope well with such a situation. Feelings don't always make sense. Jealous feelings *often* don't make sense. But if they are your feelings—or your partner's feelings—it may not be important whether or not they make sense. Feelings are feelings. They are there and we need to deal with them.

Feelings also change. Sometimes we're more "needy" and our jealous feelings are more intense. For instance, a woman who is pregnant may be bothered more with jealousy than she was earlier. Some women don't feel as attractive during pregnancy. She may think she looks fat and she may need a lot of reassurance. If her partner can't or won't give her that reassurance, she may feel very hurt over some incident he considers completely unimportant. Melodie, 16, explained her feelings:

> It was real strange because when I first went with Brett he had been going around with a lot of girls. There was always somebody hanging on to him. At first it didn't bother me—until I was pregnant. That's when it started. He'd look at girls and I'd get extremely jealous. It got so bad, so stupid—he would look at the TV and it was bad. He would look at Charlie's Angels and that bothered me! He couldn't do anything with females as far as I was concerned. He never did understand how I felt.

Lack of Self-Esteem

The biggest reason for jealousy is probably lack of self-esteem, of feeling good about oneself. If I'm bothered by my partner talking with another woman, is it because I think he'll decide he likes her better than he likes me? Do I perhaps wonder what he sees in me?

> In our marriage, jealousy hasn't been much of a problem. Before we were married, it was. Actually, I think men are very jealous, more so than women or girls. It's hard.

The idea of increased self-esteem fits it very well. Growing up, becoming more mature helps. You know, when you're in high school...teenagers are always looking at themselves and bringing out their bad points. That probably has a lot to do with jealousy among high school kids. (Derek, 18, married to Gloria, 18)

If a woman feels insecure or anxious, having her husband look at another woman might remind her that she herself isn't as desirable as she would like to be. A man who doesn't see himself as a real healthy human being is more likely to be bothered if his wife talks with another man. He may feel she is simply confirming his opinion that he isn't everything she wants.

If you are bothered with jealous feelings, it's important to try to understand what you're jealous of. What is really bothering you? If it's something that's not too hurtful to your partner, talk openly with him/her. You might say, "I feel jealous when you look at another girl. It makes me feel I'm not as pretty as she is." Open up, say how you feel about it. It's hard to bring up the subject sometimes, but it's important to do so.

Sometimes our jealous feelings may be an unconscious cover-up for our own desire to flirt. I may think, because I'm married, that I shouldn't talk to other men. If this is the case, I may have added difficulty accepting my partner feeling free to talk with other women. It's an idea you might want to discuss with your mate.

When you're talking about it, don't accuse the other person. You aren't trying to hurt your partner. Instead, you want to reflect your own feelings. "This is how I feel when I see this happen."

Ruben was married to an extremely beautiful woman. He and Shari had been together since ninth grade, but five years later he still wondered how it could last. When another man even looked at her, he got upset. And men did look at Shari.

But gradually Ruben learned to cope with these feelings. Most important was Shari's constant reassurance. She married him, she loved him. She realized he needed to be reminded of this fact, so she told him often. They shared their feelings:

Shari: *I have to remind him that I love him. It seems when we're around people, the girl gets more attention than the guys do. About half his friends are single, and I may be the only girl in the group. I have to be on my toes a lot. I have to remind him.*
Ruben: *I still find myself getting jealous because she's so beautiful, but I don't get real bothered anymore. I just talk to her*

*about it, and let her know. She talks to me and says, "Don't
worry about me." She sets me straight and I feel better.*

If you're in a partnership with a very jealous person, you may want
to help him/her get over some of those feelings. Help him/her understand that you aren't out there "looking." Your partnership is
important to you.

Trust is an important part of a good relationship. If you can start
out trusting each other, you'll be ahead. Both of you are going to be
happier if you have a high trust level.

Jealousy Related to Possessiveness

If your partner is very possessive, if s/he doesn't want the other
person to do anything alone, resentment is likely to develop:

> *He's jealous a lot—or something. I don't know what his
> problem is. He gets real upset when I want to do something with
> my sister or my friends. He doesn't have any friends or brothers.*
> (Laurie, married at 17 to Jimmy, 17)

That last comment is probably the key—"He doesn't have any
friends or brothers." Or he may simply want her home with him
because he likes to be with her.

First of all, "I don't know what his problem is" suggests that
Laurie and Jimmy should talk about it. Perhaps Laurie could include
him in more of her activities. As time passes, they may develop new
friends together.

> *We need to meet more married couples. So many of our friends
> are single. He wants to do his thing with his friends and I want to
> be with my friends. But this isn't working. We need to be
> together.* (Joni, married at 15 to Jeff, 18)

Separate friends—his and hers—can cause problems in a new
marriage. As time passes, however, most couples, if they want to,
develop friendships together. But each will probably retain some old
friends, too.

If both partners feel possessive—if neither feels good about the
other going out alone with his/her friends, both may feel fenced in.
Both may feel they are missing out on an important part of life.

Talking about these feelings is important. As each person matures, s/he may become comfortable with the other person spending time "out" with friends. If you think of marriage as a life-long commitment, you're thinking of possibly 50 or 60 years together—perhaps 70 or 80! Doing everything together could be an awful lot of togetherness.

> *I did have a problem with jealousy at one time but it wasn't getting me nowhere. So I figured if I loved him enough I could trust him. No, I'm not jealous now. I think I trust him enough.* (Marcella, married eight years ago when she was 15 to Walt, 19)

If Only One Feels Possessive

If only one partner is possessive and jealous while the other is more relaxed about outside relationships, the problem may be especially hard for both persons to handle. He may like to go out "with the boys" or spend time in the local bar. She may be very jealous of his outside relationships and want him home every night. If he stays home to please her, he may be miserable. If he ignores her wishes, she'll be miserable.

She may want to go shopping with her friends, spend more time with her family, or go to parties with her pre-marriage crowd. He thinks both should stay home. Again, whatever the solution, it may cause unhappiness—unless one or both is willing to change.

Are you with a man who expects you to stay home with the baby every night while he's out partying with his friends? "I feel..." and "How do you feel..." conversations may help. "I feel lonely here by myself night after night." "How do you feel about seeing so little of our son?" Then really listen to his answer.

Nagging him, telling him how wrong he is, probably will be no help at all. Being interested in his feelings could start a conversation which might lead to some real sharing of feelings. Sharing feelings is possible without totally agreeing with each other's point of view. This often leads to more understanding of the other person. From such understanding can come a change in attitude, or at least a compromise.

If he's been spending two or three nights per week with his friends, is he willing to cut down to one? Can you go out with him another night each week? Often you can take your child with you on visits with friends. Or you could set up baby-sitting trades with other young parents.

Of course the problem may be the opposite. You may be the man in the relationship, and you wonder why your partner wants to go out all the time. Do you think she spends too much time with her friends? With her family?

"Feelings" conversation is again a good place to start. "How do you feel about staying home?" You may find she is very lonely. Or she may dislike being home because she hates to do housework. What you thought was a refusal to be the kind of wife you wanted may instead be her way of coping with a situation she doesn't like.

How can you help? You can understand the pain of feeling lonely and discuss ways of improving the situation. If she can't stand keeping house, perhaps she needs to get a job. Then you and she can share the housework and the financial responsibilities. If she needs more education or job training, perhaps together you can work out a way for her to return to school.

The above examples may be due to possessiveness, to anxiety, or to jealousy. All three are closely related feelings. If either partner feels possessive, finding activities you can enjoy together may solve much of the problem. Gradually the possessive partner may realize it's best for each person to have interests of his/her own in addition to shared activities.

Jealousy? No problem. That goes along with trust, and you have to have trust. He goes out and he comes home and we don't argue about it. You start off with trust.

Of course, once you lose it, it won't come back right away. You have to rebuild it. But it seems to me you have to start off a relationship with trust or you wouldn't be getting into that relationship. (Dora, married at 15 to Lee, 18)

Coping with Infidelity

Sometimes jealousy is based on fact. Too often men and women leave a still-loving partner for someone else. Or s/he might have a short-term affair thinking it won't harm the primary relationship. How should this be handled?

If the straying partner leaves for the new love, the other person needs to cope as well as possible. See Chapter 12 for suggestions on dealing with this situation.

But if the straying partner says s/he really doesn't want out of your relationship, what then?

Some people immediately separate and file for divorce. "I won't put up with that," they say indignantly.

The sad part of such a situation is that sometimes the new "love" grows old very quickly. The original relationship might have a good chance of succeeding in spite of the supposed break.

The Six-Months-Rule can save marriages. Each promises the other that s/he will not make a final break from the relationship until at least six months after a problem occurs. Six months in one's lifetime isn't very long. And sometimes the problem has gone away or been resolved by the end of that six-month period. If you love someone, breaking off that relationship too quickly may be a sad mistake.

Rebuilding a trusting, loving relationship after infidelity has occurred is difficult. If the injured partner constantly brings up the incident saying, "I know I can't trust you anymore—look at what you did to me," love will be hard to regain. To forgive and forget is never easy. If you want to restore a good relationship, however, forgiving and forgetting are necessary.

If you have destroyed your partner's trust in you, you'll need to work hard on rebuilding that trust. If you plan to be faithful to him/her from now on, clearly expressing your intentions and your feelings will help. Put extra effort into demonstrating your intentions. Even more important, show your partner constantly how much you trust, respect, and care for him/her. Love can grow again if both partners are willing to work hard enough to reach this goal.

If Jealousy Is Severe

Sometimes a young man doesn't want his partner even to attend school because she "might talk to boys." Each year several girls tell me they are dropping out of high school because their husband/boyfriend doesn't want them there because there are other boys around.

If either partner is so jealous that s/he doesn't want her/his partner interacting at all with the opposite sex, a solution may be more difficult. The world is filled with both men and women. Interacting with only one sex plus one's partner is a difficult task for most of us. While some people never outgrow jealous feelings, young people tend to have a bigger problem with these feelings.

Evangelina, 18, has been married to Todd, 21, one year. She knows her jealous and anxious feelings are a real problem:

> *Todd has never had a girlfriend before except once for a week and a half. He has never lived with anybody else. I'm the only one he really knows.*
>
> *I think that's why I get jealous—because he has never experienced anything with anybody else. When he looks at other girls I get mad because I know he has never experienced anything and he may want to. I'm trying not to be jealous because if we get into big fights, that could make him want to go out and do something. Like when I tell him, "You're going to go out and do this with somebody else," he says he won't. But when I say that, it gets it into his mind. I'm trying not to say anything anymore.*
>
> *I think it's kind of childish doing what I'm doing. I'm trying not to, but I can't help it. If I look at guys, it's OK—he tells me about it, but it's OK...but if he does, I get real hyper. I just can't help myself.*

When asked if he was jealous too, Todd responded:

> *Very much so but I'm not as bad as Evangelina. When we go out someplace she's always watching me. She has to sit there and watch me to see if I'm looking at another girl. I hope she gets over it soon.*

Solving the Problem

Shauna's comments might help Evangelina:

> *I used to be a very very jealous person. Then I read this book which said you aren't hurting anybody but yourself. When you're jealous, who is hurting? Just you.*
>
> *Why should he settle for hamburger when he has steak at home? I figured if he wasn't satisfied with me but he wanted somebody else, maybe we should just split up. But we never have gone out with anybody else.*
>
> *When you're young, you don't have as much confidence in yourself as when you're older. He's a very non-jealous person. I talk to a lot of guys and he has nothing to worry about and he knows that. I used to be upset when he would talk to other girls, but now I know it's OK.* (Shauna, married at 17 to Larry, 20)

Erin, 18, married two years to Howard, 19, summed up the jealousy subject:

> *You can't live with somebody you can't trust. You've got to have honesty with each other.*

That's a big order, but many young couples find it works.

Chapter 11

> Shari: *What did it was when our daughter saw him push the table and she was scared. And our son came over and sat down and said, "I won't let Daddy hit you again, Mommy." I decided to see a counselor and Ruben agreed to go with me.*
>
> (Shari, married at 19 to Ruben, 20)

People Are Not For Hitting

*He never hits me. He knows the first time he hits me I'm
leaving. He knows I'm not going to be somebody's punching bag.
He hits the walls, but he has never hit me. A lot of girls say they
won't put up with it, and then they do stay around in spite of
being hit. But there is no way I'm going to have him hit me or
Eric.* (Jean, married at 16 to Dick, 18)

*One time he gave me a black eye when Robbie was about three
months old. My brother found out and I thought, "Oh, he's
going to kill Curt." I guess I wanted him to. But he told me,
"You guys are married now and I'd better stay out of it."*
(Annalee, married at 17 to Curt, 20)

One-third to one-half of all American women are, at some time,
beaten by their husbands or lovers. Somewhere in the United States a
woman is beaten every 15 seconds.

Of the more than 3000 teenagers surveyed for this book, almost
one-fourth of the girls and one-third of the boys said it was OK for a
husband to hit his wife, or sometimes it's necessary, or it may happen
when he's angry or drunk. Twice as many boys as girls said, "It's not
good but sometimes it's necessary." In other words, three out of ten
boys didn't see anything much wrong in men hitting women.

A slightly higher percentage of boys and girls thought it was either
OK, necessary, or OK if drunk for women to hit their husbands.

Problem More Severe for Women

People are *not* for hitting, whether male or female. The problem is
much more severe for women, however, simply because of their size
and strength as compared to men. In most situations, the man is
bigger and can hit harder than the woman. From a physical standpoint, if she hits him, he can stop her. But she can't stop him.

If a big kid hits a little kid, we call him a bully. Most of us would consider such an act wrong. Big kids aren't supposed to beat up little kids.

Then why does one-fourth to one-half of our population apparently
think it's OK for a man to beat up a woman as long as she is his wife
or girlfriend?

*I grew up with hitting, and I swear I would never put up with it
myself. I swear I would leave. My dad and my stepmother would
get drunk and he would beat her up. And the same with my*

mother and her husband. I've gotten hit quite a few times trying to stick up for her.

If it happened to me, I guess I wouldn't even try to get help for him. It's probably an illness, but I wouldn't expose my kids to that, let alone myself. Life is too short to have them go through that. (Annie, married at 15 to Jose, 17)

A group of psychology students didn't believe their college professor when he told them that many people in our society think it's perfectly all right for a man to hit his wife or girlfriend. They decided to perform an experiment to prove him wrong.

They developed three skits which they acted out in a busy shopping center. First, two young men staged a fight. Passersby stopped the skirmish immediately. Then two young women started beating on each other. Again, people walking by stopped them.

The final skit was a man beating a woman. Nobody interfered. Instead, they made comments such as "It's probably his wife," "I'll bet she deserves it," and "I wonder what she did to get herself in that situation."

The students couldn't believe it. So they repeated their experiment several times. Each time, the results were the same. If the hitting is within the family, we mustn't interfere. We act as if the marriage license is a hitting license!

Battering Compared to Rape

"I see women all the time here in the clinic who are beaten up and they really believe it is the husband's right under certain circumstances," said Van Freemon, social worker at the Whittier, California, Public Health Center. Women who are pregnant are four times as likely to be beaten as are non-pregnant women.

Ms. Freemon had been working in a Rape Crisis Center. Then, through her work at the Health Center, she began seeing battered women coming in to the Prenatal Care clinic. Somehow their stories sounded familiar. Suddenly one day it dawned on her that spouse abuse is much like rape. Rape, of course, is not a crime of sex, it is a crime of violence. Wife-beating is also a crime of violence.

Society's attitudes toward both crimes are similar, Ms. Freemon points out. Too often, it is assumed the rape victim did something to bring on the attack. It must have been because of the way she dressed or the way she walked. In the same vein, women who are beaten by their husbands run into this kind of thinking—"You must have done something to make him hit you."

A person who feels guilty herself because her husband hit her is not likely to leave him. She doesn't feel good enough about herself to be able to take that step. "The biggest problem is to deal with your own guilt. You feel embarrassed, damaged. You think you must have done something wrong. If you didn't do something wrong, you must _not_ have done something you were supposed to do," Ms. Freemon concluded.

Suzanne explained why she stayed with her husband for more than a year even though he beat her:

> _Everybody says, "If my husband ever hit me, I would leave." Well, it's not that easy. I thought I brought it on myself. I would hit him back, but I was always careful not to hurt him. But he didn't care if he hurt me. He hit hard._
>
> _But I always thought it was my fault, that I caused it. I called him names or I pushed him until I made him mad enough to hit me. But now I realize there's almost nothing you can do that is cause for that._
>
> _I finally realized he had problems, that he was really sick and it wasn't my fault. It wasn't because he hated me or even disliked me—he really loved me. I think it had a lot to do with his parents, with his dad beating him, and his mom and dad fighting. I finally realized it wasn't me and I left._ (Suzanne, married at 17 to Bill, 19)

Crisis Center Needed

Suzanne earned her high school diploma soon after her wedding. She had a good job when she finally left her husband. Most victims of spousal abuse are not so lucky. Ms. Freemon was seeing battered women at the Health Clinic who had no place to go except back to their husbands. She decided something had to be done, so she helped establish the Women's and Children's Crisis Center in Whittier.

The Center provides a safe place for women and children who are victims of domestic violence. They may stay there as long as 30 days. Counseling and other services are provided as needed.

Another tragic aspect of domestic violence is the tendency of some mothers, after being abused themselves, to take out their anger on their children. Ms. Freemon commented that soon after the Women's and Children's Crisis Center opened, they had to post a sign, "No physical punishment of children allowed." The women who were there because they had been beaten themselves were hitting their children.

"Most of them did not know how to discipline a child without beating her," she explained. The Center now holds weekly parenting classes in addition to the weekly crisis sessions. "People are not for hitting. And children are people," she said.

For a more thorough discussion of child abuse, see the relevant chapter in *Teens Parenting* (1981: Morning Glory Press).

Most women who go into the Crisis Center have nothing but the clothes they're wearing—and their kids. The house, the car, the bank account are still with the husband. What can they do?

Often they go back, only to be beaten again.

"To get into an apartment, a woman needs $1200. And in Southern California if you don't have a car, you can't work, you can't get to the store. It's extremely hard for these women," commented Ms. Freemon.

"Psychological impowerment" is the Crisis Center's goal for its clients, she explained. This means the counselors try to help each woman understand that she is important, that she has a right not to be beaten. Battered women generally have very low self-esteem.

Only by thinking badly of herself could a woman convince herself that she deserves such treatment. But she can be helped to understand her own worth, that she is a valuable person, and that nobody has a right to physically assault her. Only then does she have a chance at taking control of her life.

Which Men Batter?

How can you tell if a man is likely to beat you? We know men who batter their wives represent all ethnic groups. We know some are very poor, but others have good jobs with high incomes. Men who beat their wives often say, afterward, that they love their women.

Lenore E. Walker, author of *The Battered Woman* (1979: Harper and Row) lists some characteristics which may identify someone likely to beat his wife (p. 254):

1. Does a man report having been physically or psychologically abused as a child?
2. Was the man's mother battered by his father?
3. Has the man displayed violence against other people?

4. Does he play with guns and use them to protect himself against other people?
5. Does he lose his temper frequently and more easily than seems necessary?
6. Does he commit acts of violence against objects and things rather than people?
7. Does he drink alcohol excessively?
8. Does he display an unusual amount of jealousy when you are not with him? Is he jealous of significant other people in your life?
9. Does he expect you to spend all of your free time with him or to keep him informed of your whereabouts?
10. Does he become enraged when you do not listen to his advice?
11. Does he appear to have a dual personality?
12. Is there a sense of overkill in his cruelty or in his kindness?
13. Do you get a sense of fear when he becomes angry with you?
14. Does he have rigid ideas of what people should do that are determined by male or female sex-role stereotypes?
15. Do you think or feel you are being battered? If so, probability is high that you are a battered woman and should seek help immediately.

There are bound to be tensions and disagreements in any relationship between two people. Some men respond with violence. They may think they have a right to do so. Sometimes a man thinks of his wife as property. Most likely, he saw his father beat his mother and/or he was beaten himself as a child.

According to a study done by the San Francisco Family Violence Project, almost two-thirds of the domestic violence offenders had either seen their mothers beaten or had themselves been abused as children. Ms. Freemon goes further: "The single most important thing in wife-beating is that the man's mother was beaten by his father. Statistically, that's almost a guarantee that he's going to hit his wife," she said.

She even compares this to the fact that, if your parents speak English, you will also speak English. This is the language you learned from them. If your father beat your mother you will, if you are a man, probably beat your wife. If you are a woman, you are likely to think that is the way life is.

I have two girlfriends whose husbands always beat them. In the one, his dad always beat up his mom so he grew up thinking that was the normal thing to do. I think that's why he does. (Darci, married at 16 to Kevin, 16)

Three-Stage Cycle Described

Ms. Walker in *The Battered Woman* describes a three-stage cycle followed by men who batter their wives. The first phase she calls the "Tension-Building Phase." Tension mounts in the relationship. The woman learns to recognize signs that the cycle is starting again. He becomes more and more irritable. He can't cope with everyday stress. She will do anything possible not to annoy him during this stage. But that doesn't help because she isn't to blame. It is not her fault. His problem is within himself.

The next phase is the battering incident. At first, the batterer wants only to teach the victim a lesson. He doesn't mean to inflict injury, but in the process, he loses control of his rage. Only he can end this stage.

Sometimes a woman can guess about when this stage will end, and she leaves home until it's safe to return. She needs a place to hide during this phase. Once it's over, the victim often denies the seriousness of her injuries and the reality that this can happen again—and again.

The third stage Ms. Walker terms "Calm Respite." He becomes extremely kind and loving. He apologizes. He's afraid she will leave, so he becomes a charming model mate. Both try to convince themselves that everything will be OK from now on.

But then his inner tension begins to build again, finally to be released through another assault on his wife. The cycle is never-ending unless he is helped by expert counseling.

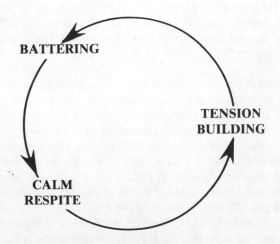

"Once a pattern of violence is started in a relationship, it almost always gets worse. He beats her more often, or more severely, or both. A battered woman lives in terror of her next beating because she knows she may not live through it," Ms. Freemon explained.

Rosemarie experienced violence while she was growing up. She realized that hitting, once it starts, seldom stops:

> *I grew up with my father knocking my sister and me around a lot. In the beginning I decided I would never put up with that. So I just walked out when it happened because I knew I didn't want it. But I didn't want to try to help him avoid the situation either.*
>
> *He didn't get mad very often but when he did, he got real mad. Usually he would punch his fist through a door rather than on us. The one time he hit me, I left.* (Rosemarie, married at 16 to Steve, 16)

Children Affected If Dad Hits Mother

Children from homes where Daddy beats Mother often have severe emotional, psychological and educational problems. They are very likely to have violent relationships themselves after they are grown.

Tricia has a son. She wanted her marriage to work. She knows it's best for a child to have two parents. But she also knew having him see his mother beaten up by his father was not a good scene.

Tricia is now divorced. She married Gary when she was 15 and he was 18. He joined the Navy and immediately went to bootcamp. For about six months she saw him only on weekends. Then he left the Navy and moved back in with his parents and Tricia went with him. She remembers:

> *It wasn't good at all. It was the same as before—getting drunk and messing around. We fought a lot and I would always come back to my mom's house. He would hit me, but no matter how hard he hit me, I would always go back to him.*
>
> *But now I think if a guy hits you once he's never going to change. If it starts with a slap, it will just get worse. If they hit once, they won't want to talk. They'll just start punching. That's the only way they have to settle things. To me there's no such thing as "He didn't mean to do it."*
>
> *At that time I didn't realize much about hitting. I thought he'd change, but now as I look back I realize there is no way he would*

change. I finally left. I couldn't handle having Louis in the middle. He was almost 18 months old when I split.

If a woman is in a marriage with a lot of violence, she should get out of it. Maybe she thinks it's her fault, but there is no reason to get slapped or punched.

Counseling May Help

Yvette is a very strong young woman. She knew that a man who hits his wife once is likely to do so again. She also knew she didn't want that kind of marriage. It took a great deal of courage to deal with it immediately:

Hitting? Some of the guys do that. When they get drunk, they feel so macho, they hit the woman. One day Vince hit me. Well, he just spanked me. I told him that was the first time and the last time. He laughed and spanked me again and I left for a week. My mom said she didn't think I should be there, but I said I had to stay there for a week.

Then one day he called me and said he was sorry that he hit me. He said that wasn't the way to fix things. Like he said, "I'm going to fix nothing by beating you up." And he never tried to do it again.

I was scared when I left. I thought if I go to my mom's house I may lose him. But if you talk to him and he doesn't understand, you have to do it some other way. (Yvette, married at 17 to Vince, 19)

Vince, a college student, also took positive action. While Yvette was at her mother's, he visited a counselor at his college. He discovered the counselor was there to help him with personal problems as well as to advise him on his class schedule. He went back several times. He said later that if Yvette hadn't gone to her mother's he wouldn't have thought he had a problem.

Yvette's action illustrates the "psychological impowerment" which, according to Ms. Freemon, is the only way a woman can really deal with abuse. If, by her action, by the way she feels about herself, she can make it perfectly clear that she will not be hit, she may cause changes in her situation.

Generally if a man hits a woman once he won't stop. It will happen again. And again. If he doesn't get professional help, he probably won't change. Even with professional help, it's hard. But, as Yvette knows, it can happen. He can change.

Characteristics of Battered Women

Ms. Freemon described a common situation: "When a battered woman comes into our Crisis Center, I ask, 'When did he start beating you?' She will say, 'About six months ago.' Then I ask, 'When was the first time he hit you?' They've been married six years and she answers, 'Six months after we were married.'

"I'll say, 'But you just said he started six months ago.' 'Oh, that's the first time he put me in the hospital.' She didn't think he was beating her if she didn't have to be hospitalized! That's a lot of denial."

Women who remain with a violent spouse tend to have some similarities, according to Ms. Freemon. At a conference presented by the Southern California Coalition on Battered Women, Ms. Freemon picked up the following list titled "Common Characteristics of Battered Women."

According to this resource a battered woman commonly:

1. Has low self-esteem.
2. Believes all the myths about battering relationships.
3. Is a traditionalist about the home—believes strongly in family unity and the prescribed feminine sex role stereotype.
4. Accepts responsibility for her partner's actions.
5. Suffers from guilt, yet denies the terror and anger she feels.
6. Seems passive, but generally manages to manipulate her environment to avoid being killed.
7. Has severe stress reactions to the point of feeling ill.
8. Uses sex as a way to establish intimacy.
9. Believes that no one will be able to help her solve her problem except herself.

Why Do They Stay?

Several young people talked about a relative or a friend who, in spite of severe beatings, stayed with the abuser. They wondered why these women didn't leave:

> *My sister got married at 18 and she already has two kids. Her husband has almost killed her several times. She tells me she stays with him because of the security. I say, "What security? He doesn't work, you support him, and he goes out with other girls right in front of you."*
>
> *They aren't very strong people, don't have much confidence in*

themselves. Everybody tries to help her and she ends up going right back to him.

If the boyfriend is violent, I would never marry him. If he hits you, then he says, "Oh, I'm sorry." But it always happens over and over again. Just like with drinking or drug usage—unless you get counseling and really work at it together, it won't stop.
(Maralee, moved in at 16 with Lyle, 16)

The reasons women give for staying in such a situation include being afraid of what the man would do to her and her children if she tried to leave him. The woman thought all along that the man would change and stop beating her. She may have had no one to turn to and she didn't know where to go for help. Perhaps she had no money and no safe place to go.

Often a woman believes she is at fault and that she has no worth as a person. She may also have believed she had to keep her husband and family together at all costs no matter what the pain and the danger.

If you or someone you know is in this kind of relationship, professional help is needed. Van Freemon cautions that many well-trained counselors are still in the "It must be her fault" mind-set. This is certainly not the kind of counseling designed to help the woman get out of a dangerous situation or to get the man into counseling. Calling a Women's Center for referrals is the best approach.

In some areas now there are temporary shelters for battered women. Staying in such a shelter can give a woman a little time for counseling and help in planning for her future. She may decide to leave her husband permanently. Or she may decide to reconcile with him after he accepts counseling.

Whatever the situation, *people are not for hitting!*

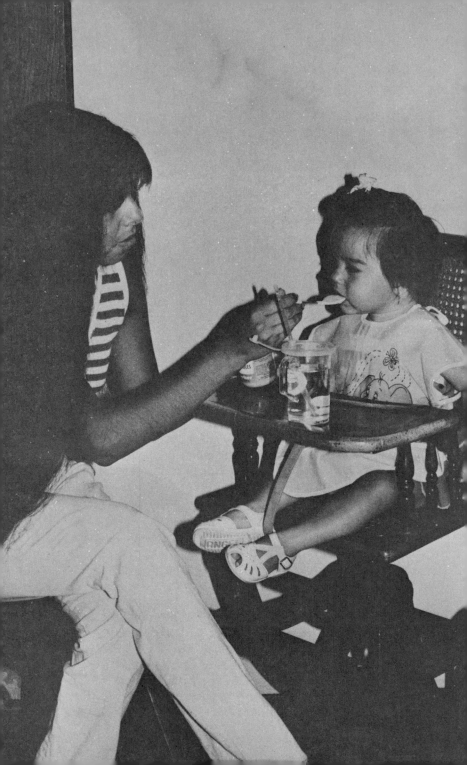

Chapter 12

Marriage is very different than I expected. I thought we would have a perfect marriage—nothing would ever go wrong. But nothing has gone right. He hasn't been able to give me the things I expected. And in return, I don't give him the things he wants.

I've tried, but I can't. I'm too bitter, too angry. I don't even like it when he comes home anymore.

(Lena, married at 16 to Tom, 18)

If It's Not Forever

> *The only way I would divorce him would be if he really hurt*
> *one of the kids or me. I've packed a few times, but I can't make*
> *myself go out the door. I have nowhere to go. I have no*
> *money—it all goes to pay the bills. I can't go back to my*
> *mother's because I'm too independent and we can't get along.*
> (Lena)

How does one decide when to give up on a marriage? Most of us
want marriage to be forever. We want a perfect marriage where
nothing will ever go wrong, as Lena expressed it. But as far as I
know, no one has ever found that perfect marriage.

It Won't Be Easy

A comment I heard often from married teenagers was, "Too many
people expect it to be easy. The first little thing that goes wrong they
think means splitting up."

This book has two purposes. One is to help young people not yet
married make a wise decision concerning this big step in their lives.
An even more important purpose is to help young people already
married and/or living together develop an even better relationship
than they have now—or at least to suggest some ways of working
together on problem areas in their marriage.

But not all marriages last. At least 60 percent of teenagers who
marry are divorced within five years. Most of these young people, no
doubt, expected their marriages to last. In the beginning they probably
said, "It won't happen to us. We're in love and we'll work out our
problems and have a wonderful life together." But time after time it
doesn't happen. Many young couples who thought marriage was their
answer are no longer together.

Just as every person is different, so is every couple's relationship
unique. No two couples were ever exactly alike. But sometimes we can
learn from another person's experience.

Many of us expect marriage to solve problems. "He'll change after
we're married." Or "She'll settle down once we're married." Trina
married Jake when she was 18. They stayed together six years, but
finally agreed to file for divorce. Trina wasn't able to change Jake as
she expected:

> *Jake resented the boys because they took my time, but I*
> *couldn't give them less. I knew when I married him that he*

wasn't good with kids, but I thought I could change him. That's the Number One thing—when you meet someone, you have to accept him as he is.

People do change, but you can't expect to change anyone but yourself. You have to accept them the way they are. I thought he would change, that he would grow into being the perfect father. But it was a real tough thing for him, and he simply didn't fit into it.

Immaturity Can Ruin Relationship

Suzanne and Bill, married at 17 and 19, are divorced. Their marriage lasted one year. Suzanne talked about their problems:

I grew up, but he didn't. He had a lot of psychological problems and didn't have any self-confidence at all. He thought he was dumb—his parents always told him he was dumb, and he dropped out of school.

I didn't realize it then, but I guess I thought I could make him feel better about himself, make him feel more important. Instead, he made me feel less important. He took away from me. He didn't want me to go to school. He didn't want me to work. But he didn't want to work either, and somebody had to work. So I was working and paying all the bills.

We didn't get married because of the pregnancy. I know he loved me and I thought I loved him. He had a lot of problems and I thought I could help him.

We moved into our apartment and lived there for a month and that month was awful, really awful. I resented the fact that he was home all day long.

It was funny—I always told myself I wouldn't worry about the house, but when I had my own place, I was just like my mom. I made sure the apartment was clean before I left. Sometimes he would still be in bed. Then when I would come home the house was a mess again.

He expected me to clean it up again, get supper, then clean up the dishes right away. He didn't do anything. Then he'd want to go someplace, but I was tired because I'd been working all day. We were constantly arguing and constantly fighting.

Suzanne's family background was quite different from Bill's. Her parents stressed the value of education. They had several children and her mother and father both worked to support their family. But Bill's mother had never worked away from home. He saw his father beat her several times. His mother's only happiness seemed to be in taking care of her only son. When he moved out with Suzanne, she was devastated. She encouraged him to move back home.

As the title of a book by Joseph W. and Lois F. Bird says, *Marriage Is for Grownups* (1971: Doubleday). If either set of parents insists on continuing to treat a married son or daughter as a spoiled child, the result is likely to be trouble for the young couple.

Counseling might have saved their marriage, but Bill was convinced he didn't have a problem. His mother reinforced his thinking, and he refused even to discuss the idea with Suzanne. She decided that, at age 16, she had made a big mistake. She didn't want to live with that mistake for the rest of her life, so she filed for divorce.

Difference in Values May Destroy Love

Matai was 16, too, when she married Jay. He was 21. They had known each other four months. She was not pregnant until several months after they married.

Several things went wrong. Because he was 21, five years older than she, he was always "in charge." She also realized they were far apart in their values, in what they wanted out of life. They had very little in common. She shared her story:

> *Before we got married he treated me half-way decent. They say love is blind and I guess I couldn't see what he was like. I partied with him a lot, but I quit after we got married. But he never stopped. He'd be out drinking and I'd be sitting up half the night waiting. I don't think that's the way marriage is supposed to be.*
>
> *After we were married he started treating me like property rather than as a human being. My sister overheard him tell his brother that a wife is supposed to have the house clean, his shoes by the door, give him a hug when he comes in, then go to bed with him!*
>
> *He was always smoking pot and drinking, and I mean every day. That's where our money went. He said he made the money and I didn't have anything to do with how it was spent.*
>
> *I think part of the reason I fell for him and married him in the first place was because I felt sorry for him because he had such a bad childhood. His mother split when he was little.*

We were together only a few months when his brother and his wife moved in. He didn't even talk to me about it. They just moved in. They'd mess up the house and I was supposed to keep it clean. But I was pregnant, and I was trying to go to school. Sometimes on Sundays they had a big barbeque and they were very messy. I'd go to bed, then go to school the next day. After school I'd come home and clean up the mess.

I kept trying to make it work, but he didn't. I kept talking to him about straightening up his act, and he said that was the way he was. If I didn't like it, I should leave. All along I pretty much knew he wasn't treating me right, but he wasn't willing to change.

I didn't put my foot down until after little Quint was born. A week after we had him, Jay wanted to take Quint over to his friends' house. They would all be smoking and drinking, so I told him no. For a week we didn't talk. Before I had always done what he said, but this time I didn't. It really shocked him and about a week later he walked out on us.

Then a few days later I called him and he came back. He said he would straighten up his act, but he lied. I think he came back for sexual reasons—you know how men are—but he stayed only two weeks, then walked out again. I filed for divorce after that.

His Reality Is Different

Of course this is an account of Matai's "reality." Jay saw their life together in a very different way:

Sure, I like to party, but I wasn't "always" drunk or high like Matai claims. I thought she liked a good time, too, when we got married, but she changed. She always wanted to stay home—especially after she got pregnant.

I suppose I should have realized she was just too young. All she could think about was going to school, coming home, and sitting here. Man, I'd go crazy with that life.

Her parents were always there, taking care of her. But she didn't want anything to do with my family. My brother and his wife drove in one day from Nebraska. I didn't know they were coming, and they needed a place to live quick. We were having trouble paying our bills, so I thought Matai would appreciate them sharing expenses. But no, she almost had a coronary.

They both found jobs right away. I thought, since Matai got

*home from school two hours before we got off work, she could
clean up the house and get supper. She didn't see it my way.*

*Then when Quint was born, I couldn't believe her. She was
really paranoid. I wanted to take the baby over to see a friend of
mine and she absolutely refused. Yes, I did walk out. I need to
have some say-so in my own home.*

Lots of problems here—but basically it was a marriage of two very
different and very young people. Matai offered some helpful final
advice:

*You should know the person a longer time. I only knew Jay for
four months. I had dated only one other person. It's probably
better to find out more about other people in the world rather
than just settling down young. Just try to keep your eyes open. If
there are things about him you don't like, do you want to put up
with that the rest of your life?*

I guèss I was pretty blind before we were married.

Counselor Cautions Against Quick Divorce

Rita Blau, clinical psychologist, works with many families at the
Intercommunity Child Guidance Center, Whittier, California. She
often talks with couples who are feeling a lot of stress in their marriages. "If there is no hope that you can make it as a couple, it's better to know that now and get on with your lives," she commented.
"But I think too many people at all age levels these days cut out too
quickly. They think it won't work so they get a divorce.

"You need to try to work things out, realize that both contribute to
the bad situation. I usually feel there is hope—there are things that
brought these two people together and let's look at those things. What
attracted them to each other in the first place? Are these things still
there and are they worth saving? What do they have to give to each
other? They both have to work at it. Sometimes it takes professional
counseling, but I'm convinced a lot of today's divorces could be
prevented."

If you aren't yet married, ask youself, "What do I want from
marriage?" Ask your partner the same question. What do you have to
give to each other? Why do you think this marriage would work? One
thing is sure. If you want a "forever" marriage, you both have to
work at it—forever.

Professional Counseling Might Help

If you and your partner are having problems, problems you don't seem to be solving on your own, perhaps professional counseling would help. Sometimes people feel they "shouldn't" need a counselor—only crazy people can't solve their own problems. Or a couple may think that if they can't get along very well, it's nobody else's business.

> *We've talked about counseling but neither of us really wants to go. If we can't work out our own problems, how can some other person help us?* (Lena)

Most people are willing to see a doctor if they break a leg or get a bad case of the flu. If they have a legal problem, they may find a good lawyer to advise them.

In the same way, a professional counselor can help an ailing marriage. Rather, the counselor can help you and your partner figure out how, through working together, you two can help your marriage improve. It's certainly not a shameful thing to see a counselor. People who do so are willing to admit they have a problem and that they would like to solve that problem.

If you want to find a counselor, ask your friends or your doctor for recommendations. Perhaps your pastor, priest or rabbi could help you. Try to find someone who appears to know what s/he is doing. S/he should be credentialed in your state as a psychologist or a marriage and family counselor.

It's best to get the names of three or four highly recommended people, then call each one and ask some questions. How long does s/he expect the counseling to continue? You probably aren't looking for years of therapy. Three or four sessions might help, or you might find you and your partner need ten or twelve appointments.

Ask about fees, and learn whether or not your health insurance will cover the charges. Does the counselor see you and your spouse separately or together? A good counselor will probably want both individual appointments and couple appointments.

If you think you and your spouse need a counselor, but your spouse refuses to go with you, what should you do? Ask the counselor's opinion. Usually they much prefer to see both persons, but are willing to see only one when necessary.

You can't change your spouse directly, and if s/he won't see the counselor with you, you may think it's an impossible situation. But you may be surprised. The counselor may help you understand your situation so much better that, even if your spouse isn't getting counseling with you, s/he will profit from your experience.

If Counseling Fails

All through this book we've been assuming that your marriage, whether now or in the future, can last forever. The underlying theme is the idea that if you and your partner work hard enough, if you trust, respect and care enough for each other, you can have a satisfying life together.

While this is what most of us want when we marry, reality for some couples is the knowledge that their marriage isn't working. In fact, the majority of teenagers fail within five years. Perhaps you and your spouse are sure your marriage isn't worth saving. What's the next step?

Good legal help is essential when you file for divorce. Cost of a lawyer's services vary tremendously.

Be as clear as possible about what you want from the lawyer before your first visit. The more visits, the more telephone calls, and the more arguments to settle between you and your spouse, the more your lawyer will charge you.

If you don't have money to pay a lawyer, check with Legal Aid in your community. Another possibility is your local Bar Association. Call either one for advice on divorce procedures.

If you and your spouse don't have any children and no property to be divided, you may be granted a divorce quickly and simply. Each state sets up its own divorce laws, however. Check the law in your state.

In some states the husband and wife are jointly responsible for any debts incurred by either one until the day the divorce is final. The divorce settlement should be very specific as to who pays which debts.

Sometimes a woman is afraid of her ex-husband. Perhaps he's threatening to take her child away from her. He might become abusive if he sees her with another man.

She needs to understand that after her divorce is final, her former spouse has no rights over her. While he may have visitation rights for their child, only through court action "for good reason" could he have the custody agreement reversed.

If he is abusive or acts in an obnoxious manner toward her, she can get a restraining order from the police which should keep him away from her.

Grief of Divorce

Perhaps to your surprise, you feel sad after your divorce. You may be positive divorce is the best thing for you. Your marriage was a big mistake, and you're eager to get on with your life. Nevertheless, you're experiencing a loss, and grief is a natural response to a loss.

In the beginning, you probably thought your marriage would last forever. Even if losing your spouse at this point is a relief, you're still losing the idea and the hope that this marriage is going to work. There will be times when you'll feel sad or confused. You may wonder if you made the right decision. Trina had some of these feelings after she and Jake were divorced:

> It was such a traumatic thing to admit defeat, that it wasn't working. I hung on to that for a long time. It still is hard. I really take it personally, and I have to try to talk myself out of it. I'd like to still be married and have a successful first marriage and have that go on forever.
>
> You take things personally when you hear people talking about working it out. But it's getting easier to where I can sit back and say, "Now wait a minute, don't start on this guilt trip."

Divorce is seldom painless. If this happens to you, talking with friends may help. Or you may decide to see a good counselor.

If a Child Is Involved

The decision to divorce is even more difficult if you have a child. You may feel it's best for a child to have two parents, but you also know continuing a bad marriage only for the sake of the child is not likely to work well either for the parents or the child.

Mothers more often than fathers are awarded custody of their children. The court, however, no longer assumes the mother should have custody. The judge makes the decision, supposedly in the best interests of the child.

Generally if the father wants visitation rights, he will be granted those rights in the divorce decree. Child support payments, if any, will also be determined in the decree.

Sometimes divorced parents decide to co-parent their children. Each may have custody on alternate weeks, for example. This takes lots of cooperation, but in some cases is a good arrangement for the child.

This setup usually works better if the parents live in the same area. A good resource is *Joint Custody and Co-Parenting Handbook* by Miriam Galper (1980: Running Press).

Even if you feel very negative about your child's father, be as positive as possible as you talk to her about him. Telling her that her father is a no-good bum could make her think she, too, is a no-good bum. You don't want that.

Should You Try Again?

Sometimes a divorced person wonders if s/he'll ever have a happy marriage. Should s/he try again? Be assured that if one marriage failed, it doesn't mean the next one will.

Some people, however, choose a second spouse remarkably like the first one. If her husband was an alcoholic, she may marry another alcoholic. If the first one spent their money foolishly, she may choose another spendthrift the second time around.

If you want to make sure this doesn't happen to you, think about the characteristics you disliked in your first husband. Think even more about the characteristics you'd like in a spouse. Your first marriage can teach you not only what you don't want in a partner but also give you a clearer idea of what you do want in your next marriage.

Include positive qualifications in your "What I want in my next marriage partner" list. You may not want someone who sits in front of the TV all evening, but what do you want? Someone who would enjoy sports with you? Someone who will be able to share your interest in music? Now's the time to think about it. Rosemarie did:

> *Being married to Bob is so different from my first marriage. Steve was pretty immature. He'd lose his temper often, and he wasn't ready to settle down. He spent most of his time in front of the TV, usually watching football games. I hated that.*
>
> *Bob and I have fun together. We like to camp out and we play tennis together. We also have plans for our future and for our kids. Right after my divorce I wondered if I'd ever have a happy marriage. Well, I found out I can.*

A person who rushes into a second marriage soon after ending the first may find earlier problems occurring again. But if each takes the time to learn as much as possible about the personality and values of the other before they marry, their relationship is more likely to last.

The Dilemma of Step-Children

When you marry again, of course your child will be involved in your plans. If he's beyond the infant stage, encourage him to talk about his feelings concerning the coming change in his life and yours.

Over and over young mothers, in speaking of a partner who is not their child's biological father, say, "He loves my child as if he were his own." And that is a reasonable goal. Rebecca wanted to make sure this would happen with Troy, 2, before she married again:

> We lived together about four months before we got married. I never thought I would be one to just live with someone, but we moved in together as a prerequisite to marriage, not just for the heck of it. I knew I wanted to be married, but I also knew I couldn't have any kind of a marriage if either Don or Troy didn't like the other. This gave us all a chance to make sure marriage was right for us.

Of course your new partner may have children too. His children, my children, and our children offer some real challenges to a relationship. Marge, 18, was pregnant when she moved in with Bill, 25. Bill's children from his first marriage, Craig, 7, and Danny, 3, spent weekends with their father. Marge had a hard time with the two boys:

> They're a mess, especially the little one. He's rude, he doesn't mind, he's wild. I can't do a thing with him. Bill won't spank him and he won't let me spank him. But what else can you do with a kid like that?

Marge needs to learn more about 3- and 7-year-old children. Normal 3-year-old children are not ready to be polite all the time. They play wildly because they have so much energy. Spanking is not a good discipline method, and a lot of parents try to avoid spanking as much as possible.

Marge and Bill could take a parenting class and learn together better ways of handling Bill's children. The important thing is that they learn together. Disagreement over children, whether ours or yours and mine, can damage an otherwise good relationship.

Divorce is difficult for everyone involved, but sometimes it's necessary. If this happens to you, get good legal advice. Make loving and responsible arrangements for your child(ren). Then get on with your life. Good luck!

Chapter 13

> *When you get married, you have to be very strong. You have to be ready for things you never thought you would ever see or ever go through. He used to tell me he needed room to breathe and he needed time to be a teenager again. He needed to find out if he wanted marriage, and I guess he discovered that was what he wanted after all. We were finally ready to settle down with each other.*

(Briann, married at 16 to Victor, 17)

Dreams & Reality... Making It Work

Briann and Victor have been married eight years. She was barely
16 and he was 17 when she became pregnant. They've had enough
problems to wreck several marriages—lack of money, living with her
parents for years, and a separation that lasted nine months. But today
they still love each other and feel very positive about their
relationship.

Her story is worth telling in some detail for several reasons. She
covers most of the topics discussed in this book—marrying very
young, marrying because of pregnancy, living with in-laws, money
problems, jealousy, wife battering (why he didn't), problems with lack
of sexual feelings after the other partner had an affair, importance of
good communication in marriage, effects of children on a relationship—this book is almost an outline of their marriage!

The most important reason for listening to Briann's story is that she
and Victor have solved so many problems. Reading about their
experiences might help someone else avoid a problem or two. That is
Briann and Victor's wish:

She's Pregnant—They Marry

*Victor and I had been dating only a few months when I
discovered I was pregnant. I was in tenth grade, barely 16. He
was a year older. For awhile, I dreaded telling him. We weren't
really that close. Finally I told him, and the first thing he said
was, "Oh, that's great. God, I can't believe it. I'll quit school
and find a job."*

*So he quit. We kept it a secret for a month, but my mother finally
found out. She and Dad had been very strict with me. I was the baby
of the family, and they thought I was still their little girl.*

*Finally Victor talked to my dad. He was very hurt and very
angry. I think what changed his viewpoint was when he asked
Victor what his intentions were. Victor said, "My intentions are
to marry her and take care of my family."*

*He got a job, but soon got fired. We waited while he looked
for something else, then decided to get married anyhow.*

*My parents went with us to the County Courthouse. His
parents didn't go because they were getting a divorce at the time,
and they didn't like me, didn't want Victor to marry me. I
remember the judge kidding around with us. We were on the
eighth floor of the courthouse and he said, "This is no time to
chicken out—it's a long drop to the ground!"*

Victor found a job and I stayed in school for awhile. Then I had some health problems and had to drop out before Andrea was born. I never went back. At that time there was no childcare at school and I really had no choice.

Living With Parents

We lived with my parents for three years. We all got along fairly well. Victor was working all that time. He was out with his friends a lot at night, but I figured that was the way men are and I'd better accept it.

I was very dependent on him—I hardly ever went anywhere by myself. When he'd get mad, I'd just sit and take his yelling. I wouldn't say a word.

My parents were very supportive. Our house has a family room and a living room, and they usually left the living room for us. We could have our friends there.

When Victor and I argued, my parents tried not to hear us. It wasn't easy for any of us, but we coped.

Victor never said anything about wishing he hadn't quit school. But he used to hate to go to work. He hardly ever complained— but he's always kept a lot inside himself.

Finally we moved to an apartment. We had it good for awhile, but then everything fell apart. We argued constantly, and I mean constantly. I knew there were arguments in every marriage, but this was too often. I figured maybe there was somebody else.

Victor Walks Out

Finally one day Victor walked out. He didn't say anything—he just walked out like he was going to the store. He didn't come back and he didn't call until the next day. All he said was he had left and he wasn't coming back.

I was shocked. About three days later it really hit me and I fell apart. I thought my whole world had ended. I depended on him for everything—income, support, company. I even depended on him to go to the store to get the things we needed. Or we'd go shopping together.

Later I realized that our relationship had been going downhill little by little. Now I think back to things going on between us,

*and I think how dumb could I be. But I never suspected it, never
thought it would happen to me.*

*So I went back to my parents. I assumed they would welcome
me back, that they would take care of me and Andrea. But my
dad said, "No, I love you very much, but I'm not going to give
him the satisfaction of having me raise his family. You get off
your butt and go over to welfare."*

*So the next day I went to welfare. They asked me a lot of questions.
Then they called Victor in and he started paying child support.*

She's Pregnant Again

*To make it harder, I was pregnant again. He didn't know it
and my parents didn't know either.*

*I decided I had to have an abortion. I made the appointment
and paid my money. But when I got on the table, I suddenly
realized I would regret this the rest of my life. So I told them to
stop. I got off the table and sat for two hours while the
anesthesia wore off.*

*I came home and felt like a whole new thing had happened to
me. I told myself I would be damned if I would let him ruin my
life. I decided to take charge.*

*Finally I told my parents I was pregnant and my Dad said he
would help me. I told him no, that I was going to make it by
myself. But Andrea and I continued to live with them.*

*Victor came over to my parents' house for lunch a lot so he
could see Andrea. Most of the time I wasn't there. I'd go over to
my brother's. I couldn't handle being with him. Each time he
left, I was afraid I'd say, "Don't leave, come back." But I didn't
want to beg him.*

*Andrea was four when he left, and her Dad was her whole
world. She stopped talking to me for about three months because
she thought I had kicked him out. Finally I had him sit down and
tell her what had happened.*

*I had been with my parents six or seven months when I went
into labor with Vince. I didn't want to call Victor but my parents
were gone. Finally I tried to reach him, but he wasn't home.
Then my parents came home and took me to the hospital. I was
in labor for 12 hours, and I told them not to call him. Finally
Mom did. I had the security guard throw him out while I was in
the labor room. He came over after Vince was born.*

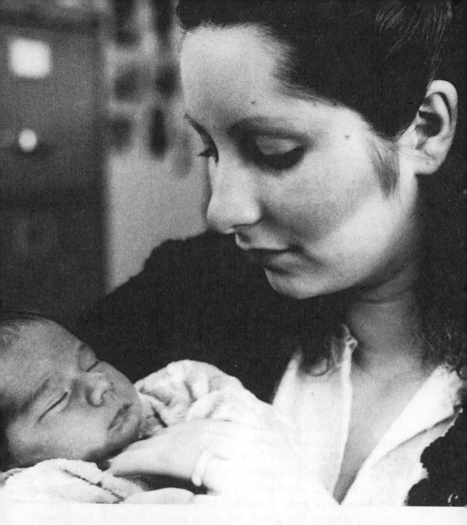

We continued living with my parents. By then I knew Victor was having an affair with another girl. I didn't know her and never saw them together until one day I went to the park with the kids. There he was with her. Andrea was upset and so was I. I told him, "I can't handle this. It's not so much what you're putting me through, but what you're doing to our kids."

Briann Leaves Town

I decided I had to get out of there. My sister was in Stockton, so I took the kids there. I didn't tell Victor we were leaving. The next day he came over and my Dad told him. He was furious.

*Two weeks after we got to Stockton, Victor started calling me.
He called me over and over and told me he wanted us back. He
had thought he wanted his freedom but he knew now he didn't.
That life wasn't for him, he said.*

*I told him he could come back only under my conditions.
"You stepped all over me and I don't want that," I told him. He
kept calling, and I finally came home. He came over and I laid
down my conditions. I said, "You won't go out with your friends
after work. If you go to a party, make sure it's a party where you
can take your wife."*

*I also said we couldn't live with my parents. I said if we got
back together, we had to start fresh by ourselves. I told him to go
back to his apartment and think about it—that if he came back
through that door, he was going to leave his affairs behind.*

Making a Second Start

*The next day he came back. He said he was sorry and that he
had decided to be a man for his family. At that time he was 22
and I was 21.*

*We moved out a week or two later. We figured we needed time
on our own, privacy to straighten out what we had messed up.
We had some rough times—it wasn't the same. It could never be
the same. After we were back together I just couldn't
communicate like a husband and wife. It took us a good year to
get back to being close again.*

*It's been three years now, and he's still working on his relation-
ship with Andrea. He'll ask her to do something and she'll look
at me first. If he goes skiing with his friends overnight, the first
thing she says is, "Where's my Dad? Is he gone?"*

*During the months we were separated, her grades in school
were much worse. After we got back together, they went up
again. We didn't get back together because of the kids, but we
knew they needed us both.*

*Our whole life changed. The togetherness, the loving took a
long time to come back. But I could feel the environment around
us had changed.*

*When he came back he said, "You have really grown up. I
don't know whether it's because I hurt you or what." I said I
thought it was from having a baby by myself and not having the
father around like he ought to be.*

Finally She Can Argue

He was very surprised at the times I would yell back—I never used to do that. Before, he would go on and on about something. I would just sit there. He did the yelling. But now I yell back, and it really shocks him. Now lots of times he drops the subject. He doesn't care to continue it.

If you don't argue in a marriage, you aren't communicating at all. You have got to let your feelings and your anger out. We both have found we're better off doing that.

At least he didn't beat on me like a couple of our neighbors' husbands do on them. Once while we were separated, I hit him. He was shocked that I did it. He had accused me of going out with somebody and I got very mad. When he was mad he used to yell a lot—or he would walk outside and stay there. He was a battered child until he was 16 and let his father have it. His father beat his mother, and Victor grew up knowing that wasn't right.

He doesn't spank his kids. Sometimes that bothers me because I think they may need it. But he would rather talk to them. He says he never wants that life for his kids, and I'm glad.

Trust—Hard to Regain

Sometimes he tells me, "I know you aren't very trusting of me." I say, "How would you feel if it were the other way around?" He thinks, then says, "You know, I don't think I could trust you." I would like to trust him, and I do mostly. We have a good relationship now, but I don't want the same things to come up that were coming up before.

We talked a lot about those months we were apart. Sometimes I was even able to kid him about his girlfriend. "I don't even want to think about it," he would say. "I wasted nine months of my life messing around like a teenage boy." But we were so young when we got married, never much time to go out with other people, to enjoy our friends, our freedom.

I think our breakup was the best thing that ever happened to us, I really do. We have gotten closer together, more open. We can argue to where I can yell back. Before I would just hold back because I was always afraid to say something because he would storm out. Sometimes we argue and we start laughing at each other because the whole thing is so ridiculous.

She's Less Dependent

*I don't depend on him very much now, at least not like I used
to. Sometimes I get scared that this might happen again. But I
tell myself that if it does, I can manage. I doubt if I would go
back again. I don't think I could go through all that hurt again.
I thought I was going to die. I thought my whole life had ended.*

*I think there was enough love to make us both hang in there. I
don't really know how I managed. I used to tell him I feel like I
aged ten years in those nine months. You really grow up fast.*

*I didn't get professional help. Instead I sat and thought a lot.
It's a two-way deal—you both have to be willing. If you aren't, it
won't work.*

*There's really not one way of making a marriage work because
people are so different. Everybody has their own ways of seeing
things. Some people give up and just say forget it. I'm glad we
didn't do that.*

*Even my dad says, "Victor has changed a lot. He's a family
man now and I give him a lot of credit. He makes me proud to
say he's my son-in-law."*

*We honestly enjoy each other's company now. Before, we
couldn't stand being together a lot of the time. We go to parties
together now and we have a lot of the same interests. We like
some of the same sports.*

*Recently we got into skiing and I really love it. We bike and go
bowling. He's into baseball but I don't like to play so I watch.
Now he's starting to play golf, too. He wanted me to play but I
can't see hitting a ball, then walking to see where it went. We
joined a health spa last month and we go together twice a week.*

*Things have really worked out. I thank God that we made it
out of that mess OK. I think it would have been hard for me to
find somebody else with my two kids. My first question would
be, "Would that man love my kids as much as their father loves
them?" It's really something to think about before divorcing and
making it final. There is a lot of hurt, a lot of memories for kids
when their parents split.*

Explaining to Andrea

*Andrea was always asking me questions because her friends
say, "Your mother is so young." She wanted to know how old I*

was when I got married. Finally I sat down and told her about our early marriage and about my pregnancy.

I told her if she got pregnant I wouldn't turn her out and I wouldn't push her into giving the baby up. But I also told her I wouldn't suggest she get married right away. I would recommend living apart, or perhaps moving in together for a year—but getting to know her feelings. Getting married is a very big step—it's for the rest of your life.

If you get a divorce, that hangs over your head forever. Before you get married, get to know his ways. Make sure he treats you good, and see that he's supportive of you and that baby you're going to have.

I worry so much for her, maybe because times are getting harder now. Income isn't going as far as it should. How is it going to be when she gets to the age we were when we started?

She and her cousins have dreams of getting jobs, buying big cars, and living good. I had dreams, too. I wanted to be an airline stewardess—I had all sorts of dreams. But I didn't stick with those dreams. I got involved with Victor and I got pregnant. I don't tell her I regret it, but I do encourage her in her dreams.

Building a good marriage is a difficult and never-ending task. Briann and Victor gave up briefly, then decided to try again. Their life together now is better than ever.

The road to a forever marriage is never easy, but if it's paved with trust, respect and caring, *your* love can find a way. Good luck and best wishes on *your* journey.

Appendix

SCORECARD FOR PREDICTING SUCCESS
OF TEENAGE MARRIAGE

Love, based on trust, respect, and caring, is the most important ingredient of a good marriage, but it is impossible to measure these very special ingredients. Other important factors in developing a lasting marriage can be measured, however. The following questions are designed to measure your partner's and your readiness for marriage. Your score can give you a rough estimate of your chances for a successful marriage. Answer the following questions *honestly* by circling the number (1, 2, 3, 4, or 5) of your answer—or write the numbers on another sheet of paper. Then ask your partner to answer the questions. Do your scores match?

1. How old are you?
   1. Sixteen   2. Seventeen   3. Eighteen   4. Nineteen   5. Twenty or older
2. How old is your partner?
   1. Sixteen   2. Seventeen   3. Eighteen   4. Nineteen   5. Twenty or older
3. What is the highest grade in school you have completed?
   1. Grade 10   2. Grade 11   3. Grade 12   4. Grade 13   5. Grade 14
4. What is the highest grade in school your partner has completed?
   1. Grade 10   2. Grade 11   3. Grade 12   4. Grade 13   5. Grade 14
5. Do you and your partner belong to the same ethnic group?
   3. No   5. Yes
6. Do you and your partner agree on religion?
   1. Disagree completely   2. Disagree somewhat   3. It's not important to us
   4. Mostly agree   5. Agree completely
7. Are your family backgrounds pretty much alike?
   1. Not at all   3. Somewhat alike   5. Very much alike
8. On a scale of 1 to 5, how good do you feel about yourself?
   Not good at all—1—2—3—4—5—Very good (high self-esteem)
9. On a scale of 1 to 5, how good does your partner feel about him/herself?
   Not good at all—1—2—3—4—5—Very good (high self-esteem)
10. How long have you known each other?
    1. 1-3 months   2. 3-6 months   3. 6-12 months   4. 12-18 months   5. 18 months or more
11. Are you (or is your partner) pregnant?   2. Yes   5. No
12. On a scale of 1 to 5, how well do you and your partner agree on how many children you want and when you want them?
    Don't agree at all—1—2—3—4—5—Agree perfectly
13. On a scale of 1 to 5, how do you feel about your partner's parents?
    I don't like them at all—1—2—3—4—5—Think they're wonderful
14. On a scale of 1 to 5, how does your partner feel about your parents?
    Doesn't like them at all—1—2—3—4—5—Thinks they're wonderful

15. Is either of you marrying to escape a bad family situation?
    1. Yes 5. No

16. Does either of you think the other one has a drug or alcohol problem? 1. Yes 5. No

17. On a scale of 1 to 5, how jealous are you and your partner of each other?
    Terribly jealous—1—2—3—4—5—We trust each other completely

18. How much do you and your partner argue?
    1. Constantly 3. Never 5. Occasionally

19. How many interests/activities do you share with your partner?
    1. One 2. Two 3. Three 4. Four 5. Five or more

20. Does either or both of you have a good job now?
    1. Neither one 2. No, but one is in school 3. No, but both are in school
    4. Yes, one of us 5. Yes, both of us

21. On a scale of 1 to 5, how well do you and your partner agree on how you spend your money?
    We don't agree at all—1—2—3—4—5—We almost always agree

22. How do you and your partner feel about traditional versus equal marriage as defined in Chapter 6?
    1. We don't agree 3. We both want a traditional marriage
    5. We both want an equal marriage

23. On a scale of 1 to 5, how well do you and your partner communicate with each other?
    Poorly—1—2—3—4—5—Very well

Now total your score. If it's between 100 and 115, you and your partner have a lot going for you. Good luck!

If you score 90-99, you'll need to work at your marriage a little harder.

If you score 80-89, be careful. You're likely to have a rough time if you get married now.

Is your score between 70 and 79? How about postponing your decision for at least a year?

If you score below 70, you two don't appear to have much going for you. Please consider looking for someone else—or at least postponing your decision for quite a while.

Of course there is no measure that will guarantee either a happy marriage or a bad one. This scorecard is designed simply to help you and your partner consider some crucial factors involved in making perhaps the most important decision of your life. Please think carefully!

WHAT ARE YOUR ATTITUDES TOWARD MARRIAGE?

The marriage attitudes survey often mentioned in this book included a number of descriptive questions, questions designed to provide information about the survey group. Most of the 118 questions, however, dealt directly with attitudes toward marriage.

You might find that answering and discussing these 100 questions with your partner would help each of you understand better how the other feels about various issues. It would be best for each of you to answer all of the questions alone, then share your answers. The results may surprise you.

Permission is granted to make copies of the questionnaire in order to make it easier to use. If you copy it, simply circle on your copy the letter of the answer of your choice. Otherwise, you and your partner could each number 1 to 100 on a sheet of paper, then write the letter of your chosen answer next to the appropriate number.

Remember—discussing your answers together may help you understand each other more completely.

How much do you think getting married at age 18 or younger would change your life in the following areas? (If you are already married, how has marriage changed your life?)

1. MONEY:
   A. I'd have more money.   B. I'd have less money.   C. No change.
2. FRIENDS:
   'A. More friends.   B. Fewer friends.   C. Different friends.   D. No change.
3. RECREATION/PARTYING: A. More.   B. Less.   C. No change.
4. FREE TIME: A. More.   B. Less.   C. No change.
5. RELATIONSHIP WITH YOUR FAMILY:
   A. Closer.   B. Less close.   C. No change.
6. HIGH SCHOOL ATTENDANCE:
   A. I'd drop out.   B. I'd continue going to school.
   C. I would graduate.   D. Marriage wouldn't change my attendance.
7. COLLEGE/TRADE SCHOOL:
   'A. I'd be more likely to attend.   B. Less likely to attend.   C. No change.
8. Do you want to marry a person from your own ethnic group or race?   A. Absolutely.   B. Probably.   C. It doesn't matter.
   D. Probably not.   E. Absolutely not.
9. Do you think marrying a person from a different ethnic group would usually cause problems within a marriage?   A. Absolutely.
   B. Probably.   C. I don't know.   D. Probably not.   E. Absolutely not.
10. Do you want to marry a person who has the same religious beliefs as you do?   A. Absolutely.   B. Probably.   C. It doesn't matter.
    D. Probably not.   E. Absolutely not.

11. Do you think marrying a person with a religious faith different from your own would cause problems in your marriage?
A. Absolutely. B. Probably. C. I don't know.
D. Probably not. E. Absolutely not.

12. Do you want your marriage to be much like your parents' marriage? A. Absolutely. B. Probably. C. It doesn't matter.
D. Probably not. E. Absolutely not.

13. When you get married, do you expect it to last the rest of your life? A. Absolutely. B. Probably. C. It doesn't matter.
D. Probably not. E. Absolutely not.

14. How is your relationship with your mother?
A. Very good. B. Good. C. Fair D. Poor. E. No relationship.

15. How is your relationship with your father?
A. Very good. B. Good. C. Fair. D. Poor. E. No relationship.

16. How do you feel about a young couple living with either his or her parents? A. Good idea. B. OK until we save some money.
C. I would rather not. E. I'm totally against it.

17. How do you feel about a man and woman living together if they aren't married? A. It's OK. B. It's OK if they plan to get married later.
C. It's OK but I wouldn't do it. D. I think it's wrong.

18. If you have a problem, to whom do you talk?
A. Nobody. B. Parents C. Teacher, counselor, or minister.
D. Another friend. E. Boy/Girlfriend (or husband/wife).

19. When a couple has an argument, who should usually have the final say? A. Male. B. Female. C. It doesn't matter.

20. If you are upset with your partner, what do you do? (more than one answer is OK.) A. Tell him/her you are upset. B. Hit him/her.
C. Leave and think it through. D. Tell a friend or parent, but not your partner.
E. I don't do anything.

21. When you and your boyfriend/girlfriend have an argument, how do you settle it? (More than one answer is OK.) A. Slug it out.
B. Talk it through together. C. Yell to get rid of bad feelings.
D. Quit talking to each other. E. Get a referee.

22. How do you feel about husbands hitting their wives? A. It's OK.
B. It's not good, but sometimes it's necessary. C. It should never happen.
D. It's not OK, but it may happen when he's angry or drunk.

23. How do you feel about wives hitting their husbands? A. It's OK.
B. It's not good, but sometimes it's necessary. C. It should never happen.
D. It's not OK, but it may happen when she's angry or drunk.

In a *good* marriage, who should be responsible for the following tasks?

24. EARNING MONEY:
A. Husband. B. Wife. C. Both. D. It doesn't matter.

25. DECIDING HOW MONEY IS SPENT:
A. Husband. B. Wife. C. Both. D. It doesn't matter.

26. PAYING BILLS:
    A. Husband.   B. Wife.   C. Both.   D. It doesn't matter.
27. VACUUMING THE HOUSE:
    A. Husband.   B. Wife.   C. Both.   D. It doesn't matter.
28. MOPPING FLOORS:
    A. Husband.   B. Wife.   C. Both.   D. It doesn't matter.
29. PREPARING MEALS:
    A. Husband.   B. Wife.   C. Both.   D. It doesn't matter.
30. CLEANING UP AFTER MEALS:
    A. Husband.   B. Wife.   C. Both.   D. It doesn't matter.
31. WASHING THE CAR:
    A. Husband.   B. Wife.   C. Both.   D. It doesn't matter.
32. MOWING THE LAWN:
    A. Husband.   B. Wife.   C. Both.   D. It doesn't matter.
33. PLAYING WITH THE CHILDREN:
    A. Husband.   B. Wife.   C. Both.   D. It doesn't matter.
34. FEEDING BABIES/CHILDREN:
    A. Husband.   B. Wife.   C. Both.   D. It doesn't matter.
35. CHANGING BABY'S DIAPERS:
    A. Husband.   B. Wife.   C. Both.   D. It doesn't matter.
36. DISCIPLINING CHILDREN:
    A. Husband.   B. Wife.   C. Both.   D. It doesn't matter.
37. BATHING BABY:
    A. Husband.   B. Wife.   C. Both.   D. It doesn't matter.
38. PUTTING BABY TO BED:
    A. Husband.   B. Wife.   C. Both.   D. It doesn't matter.
39. PUTTING TODDLER TO BED:
    A. Husband.   B. Wife.   C. Both.   D. It doesn't matter.
40. DOING FAMILY'S LAUNDRY:
    A. Husband.   B. Wife.   C. Both.   D. It doesn't matter.
41. Is sex an important part of marriage?
    A. Absolutely.   B. Probably.   C. I don't know.
    D. Probably not.   E. Absolutely not.
42. Do you think a couple should have sexual intercourse before they
    are married?   A. Absolutely.   B. Probably.   C. It doesn't matter.
    D. Probably not.   E. Absolutely not.
43. When a high school-age girl gets pregnant, should she and her
    boyfriend get married?
    A. Absolutely.   B. Probably.   C. It doesn't matter.
    D. Probably not.   E. Absolutely not.
44. Do you think it is important for a child to live with both of
    his/her parents?   A. Absolutely.   B. Probably.
    C. It doesn't matter.   D. Probably not.   E. Absolutely not.
45. For how long have you lived with both of your parents?
    A. All my life.   B. 10-15 years.   C. 5-10 years.   D. 0-5 years.   E. Never.
46. Do you think having "enough" money is an important part of a
    good marriage?   A. Absolutely.   B. Probably.
    C. It doesn't matter.   D. Probably not.   E. Absolutely not.

47. Do you think it is important for a husband and wife to agree on how they spend money? A. Absolutely. B. Probably. C. I don't know. D. Probably not. E. Absolutely not.

48. Do you think it is important for a husband and wife to agree on how to discipline their children? A. Absolutely. B. Probably. C. I don't know. D. Probably not. E. Absolutely not.

49. If you were married, would you want your spouse to continue his/her education? A. Absolutely. B. Probably. C. It doesn't matter. D. Probably not. E. Absolutely not.

50. Do you think being married would tie you down? A. Absolutely. B. Probably. C. I don't know. D. Probably not. E. Absolutely not.

51. In a good marriage, should the husband earn most of the money? A. Absolutely. B. Probably. C. It doesn't matter. D. Probably not. E. Absolutely not.

52. In a good marriage, should the wife be a good housekeeper? A. Absolutely. B. Probably. C. It doesn't matter. D. Probably not. E. Absolutely not.

53. In a good marriage, should the husband take care of the car and lawn? A. Absolutely. B. Probably. C. It doesn't matter. D. Probably not. E. Absolutely not.

54. In a good marriage, should the wife do most of the cooking? A. Absolutely. B. Probably. C. It doesn't matter. D. Probably not. E. Absolutely not.

FOR BOYS ONLY: (Girls—Please skip 55-66)

55. Do you expect your wife to work outside your home until you have children? A. Absolutely. B. Probably. C. It doesn't matter. D. Probably not. E. Absolutely not.

56. Do you expect your wife to work outside your home while you have children under two years of age? A. Absolutely. B. Probably. C. It doesn't matter. D. Probably not. E. Absolutely not.

57. Do you expect your wife to work outside your home after your children are all in school? A. Absolutely. B. Probably. C. It doesn't matter. D. Probably not. E. Absolutely not.

58. Would it be all right with you if your wife wanted to get a job? A. Absolutely. B. Probably. C. I don't know. D. Probably not. E. Absolutely not.

59. Would it be all right with you if your wife made more money than you? A. Absolutely. B. Probably. C. I don't know. D. Probably not. E. Absolutely not.

60. Would it be all right with you if your wife chose to stay home instead of getting a job? A. Absolutely. B. Probably. C. I don't know. D. Probably not. E. Absolutely not.

FOR GIRLS ONLY: (Boys—Please skip 61-66.)

61. Do you expect to work outside your home until you have children?
    A. Absolutely.   B. Probably.   C. It doesn't matter.
    D. Probably not.   E. Absolutely not.

62. Do you expect to work outside the home while you have children under two years of age?
    A. Absolutely.   B. Probably.   C. It doesn't matter.
    D. Probably not.   E. Absolutely not.

63. Do you expect to work outside your home after your children are all in school?
    A. Absolutely.   B. Probably.   C. It doesn't matter.
    D. Probably not.   E. Absolutely not.

64. Would it be all right with you if your husband said you should *not* get a job?
    A. Absolutely.   B. Probably.   C. I don't know.
    D. Probably not.   E. Absolutely not.

65. Would it be all right with you if your husband said you *must* get a job?
    A. Absolutely.   B. Probably.   C. I don't know.
    D. Probably not.   E. Absolutely not.

66. Would it be all right with you if your *husband* wanted to stay home while you got a job to support your family?
    A. Absolutely.   B. Probably.   C. I don't know.
    D. Probably not.   E. Absolutely not.

FOR BOYS ONLY: (Girls—Please skip 67-78.)

WOULD YOU BE JEALOUS IF YOUR GIRLFRIEND OR WIFE:

67. Looked at other boys?
    A. Absolutely.   B. Probably.   C. I don't know.
    D. Probably not.   E. Absolutely not.

68. Talked with other boys?
    A. Absolutely.   B. Probably.   C. I don't know.
    D. Probably not.   E. Absolutely not.

69. Worked with boys?
    A. Absolutely.   B. Probably.   C. I don't know.
    D. Probably not.   E. Absolutely not.

70. Went to school with boys?
    A. Absolutely.   B. Probably.   C. I don't know.
    D. Probably not.   E. Absolutely not.

71. Went to a concert with another boy?
    A. Absolutely.   B. Probably.   C. I don't know.
    D. Probably not.   E. Absolutely not.

72. Had a close male friend?
    A. Absolutely.   B. Probably.   C. I don't know.
    D. Probably not.   E. Absolutely not.

FOR GIRLS ONLY: (Boys—Please skip 73-78.)

WOULD YOU BE JEALOUS IF YOUR BOYFRIEND OR YOUR HUSBAND:

73. Looked at other girls?
    A. Absolutely. B. Probably. C. I don't know.
    D. Probably not. E. Absolutely not.

74. Talked with other girls?
    A. Absolutely. B. Probably. C. I don't know.
    D. Probably not. E. Absolutely not.

75. Worked with girls?
    A. Absolutely. B. Probably. C. I don't know.
    D. Probably not. E. Absolutely not.

76. Went to school with girls?
    A. Absolutely. B. Probably. C. I don't know.
    D. Probably not. E. Absolutely not.

77. Went to a concert with another girl?
    A. Absolutely. B. Probably. C. I don't know.
    D. Probably not. E. Absolutely not.

78. Had a close female friend?
    A. Absolutely. B. Probably. C. I don't know.
    D. Probably not. E. Absolutely not.

FOR BOYS *AND* GIRLS: HOW IMPORTANT DO YOU THINK IT IS FOR A *HUSBAND* TO HAVE THE FOLLOWING QUALITIES?

79. Good money manager.
    A. Very important. B. Somewhat important.
    C. Not important. D. It doesn't matter at all.

80. Loves and cares about children.
    A. Very important. B. Somewhat important.
    C. Not important. D. It doesn't matter at all.

81. Good cook.
    A. Very important. B. Somewhat important.
    C. Not important. D. It doesn't matter at all.

82. Good housekeeper.
    A. Very important. B. Somewhat important.
    C. Not important. D. It doesn't matter at all.

83. Knows how to repair the plumbing.
    A. Very important. B. Somewhat important.
    C. Not important. D. It doesn't matter at all.

84. Doesn't get upset easily.
    A. Very important. B. Somewhat important.
    C. Not important. D. It doesn't matter at all.

85. Takes care of the yard.
    A. Very important. B. Somewhat important.
    C. Not important. D. It doesn't matter at all.

86. Takes charge of home and family.
    A. Very important. B. Somewhat important.
    C. Not important. D. It doesn't matter at all.

87. Good sex partner.
   A. Very important.   B. Somewhat important.
   C. Not important.   D. It doesn't matter at all.

88. Shares common interests with spouse.
   A. Very important.   B. Somewhat important.
   C. Not important.   D. It doesn't matter at all.

89. Spends most of his spare time with his spouse.
   A. Very important.   B. Somewhat important.
   C. Not important.   D. It doesn't matter at all.

FOR BOYS *AND* GIRLS: HOW IMPORTANT DO YOU THINK IT IS FOR A *WIFE* TO HAVE THE FOLLOWING QUALITIES?

90. Good money manager.
   A. Very important.   B. Somewhat important.
   C. Not important.   D. It doesn't matter at all.

91. Loves and cares about children.
   A. Very important.   B. Somewhat important.
   C. Not important.   D. It doesn't matter at all.

92. Good cook.
   A. Very important.   B. Somewhat important.
   C. Not important.   D. It doesn't matter at all.

93. Good housekeeper.
   A. Very important.   B. Somewhat important.
   C. Not important.   D. It doesn't matter at all.

94. Knows how to repair the plumbing.
   A. Very important.   B. Somewhat important.
   C. Not important.   D. It doesn't matter at all.

95. Doesn't get upset easily.
   A. Very important.   B. Somewhat important.
   C. Not important.   D. It doesn't matter at all.

96. Takes care of the yard.
   A. Very important.   B. Somewhat important.
   C. Not important.   D. It doesn't matter.

97. Takes charge of home and family.
   A. Very important.   B. Somewhat important.
   C. Not important.   D. It doesn't matter at all.

98. Good sex partner.
   A. Very important.   B. Somewhat important.
   C. Not important.   D. It doesn't matter at all.

99. Shares common interests with spouse.
   A. Very important.   B. Somewhat important.
   C. Not important.   D. It doesn't matter at all.

100. Spends most of her spare time with her spouse.
   A. Very important.   B. Somewhat important.
   C. Not important.   D. It doesn't matter at all.

ANNOTATED BIBLIOGRAPHY

Many books are available in which marriage in general is discussed. More than 500 titles are listed under "Marriage" in the current edition of *Books in Print*. Quite a few resources concerned with teenage pregnancy and parenthood have been published. However, there are very few books dealing directly with teenage marriage. In fact, the same edition of *Books in Print* lists only three under "Teenage Marriage."

The following bibliography includes the books mentioned in *Teenage Marriage: Coping with Reality*. Also listed are some especially good titles for and about pregnant adolescents and school-age parents. A few novels with a teenage marriage theme are included. Easy readability, high interest level, and practicality of information were the major criteria for selection of titles.

Prices quoted are from *Books in Print*, 1983. Because prices change so rapidly, however, and because publishers move, it is wise to call your local library reference department for an updated price and address before ordering a book. Most publishers add a handling charge of $1.50 — $2.00 for books ordered by mail.

Barr, Linda, and Catherine Monserrat. *Teenage Pregnancy: A New Beginning.* 1978. New Futures, Inc., 2120 Louisiana NE, Albuquerque, NM 87110. $10.00. Spanish edition available. Quantity discount.

A book written specifically for pregnant adolescents, this is an excellent 80-page illustrated textbook. Topics include prenatal health care, nutrition during pregnancy, fetal development, preparation for labor and delivery, decision-making, emotional effects of adolescent pregnancy, and others. The authors have obviously known, worked with, and loved many school-age parents. The book is written for them and often quotes them. It is written at a sixth grade reading level.

_____ . *Working with Childbearing Adolescents: A Guide for Use with Teenage Pregnancy, A New Beginning.* New Futures, Inc. $10.00.

This book is designed specifically for professionals who work with pregnant adolescents. The introductory chapter presents an overview of teen pregnancy and parenthood in the United States. In addition, adolescent development and sexuality are explored. The book also contains a complete course outline with lesson plans and resource material to accompany each chapter in the student text. Learning strategies are applicable both to classroom and to individualized study. The authors have included their experiences, ideas, and insights gained through working with pregnant adolescents.

Bayard, Robert T., Ph.D., and Jean Bayard, Ph.D. *How to Deal with Your Acting-Up Teenager: Practical Self-Help for Desperate Parents.* 1981. 205 pp. $11.95. M. Evans & Co., 216 E. 49th St., New York, NY 10017.

As the title implies, this book was written for parents of teenagers. It is also an excellent resource for other people working with adolescents.

Bird, Joseph W., and Lois F. Bird. *Marriage Is for Grownups.* 1971. $4.50. Doubleday & Co., Inc., 501 Franklin Ave., Garden City, NY 11530.

The authors offer suggestions for improving relations between husband and wife. They discuss such problems as inadequate communication, money, sex, relatives, infidelity, children, vacations, and religion.

Broderick, Carlfred. *Couples: How to Confront Problems and Maintain Loving Relationships.* 1981. Touchstone Books. $5.95. Simon & Schuster, Inc., 1230 Avenue of the Americas, New York, NY 10020.

Couples is an informative, warm, and helpful book for married couples and for any two people living together. Dr. Broderick covers topics ranging from "emotional space" and dependency to infidelity to coping with children. Many discussions from actual counseling sessions are included.

Edens, David. *Marriage: How to Have It the Way You Want It.* 1982. Prentice-Hall, Inc., Englewood Cliffs, NJ 07632. $5.95.

A psychologist and family therapist, David Edens offers practical, structured exercises and activities for any man or woman seeking to open communication and enrich a present or future marriage. Specific topics include companionship, vocational compatibility, sexual satisfaction, and others.

Bode, Janet. *Kids Having Kids: The Unwed Teenage Parent.* 1980. 107 pp. $7.90. Franklin Watts, Inc., 387 Park Avenue South, New York, NY 10019.

The book focuses on experiences of young women and their attitudes toward sexuality, pregnancy, birth control, abortion, and the role of father. A brief discussion of teenage marriage is included.

Foster, Sallie. *The One Girl in Ten.* 1981. Arbor Press, Box 846, Claremont, CA 91711. $5. 10/more, $4. Shipping: 1—2, $1; 3—6, $2; 7—10, $3.

Sally Foster, retired social worker, taped interviews with 126 school-age mothers. The One Girl in Ten is the result of these interviews. These young mothers tell their stories with the utmost frankness from their first experience with sex through the anxious months of pregnancy to the period after childbirth. One chapter is titled "Marriage as a Solution."

Furstenberg, Frank F., Jr. *Unplanned Parenthood: The Social Consequences of Teenage Childbearing.* 1979. $8.95. Free Press, 866 Third Avenue, New York, NY 10022.

A six-year study of 400 adolescent mothers was done in Baltimore from 1966 — 1972. Results of the study, detailed in this book, present solid statistics to back up the following conclusion: "The adolescent mothers consistently experienced great difficulty in realizing their life plans, when compared with their classmates who did not become pregnant premaritally in their early teens." The study focused not only on the 400 young mothers, but also on their partners, children, and parents. It also compared the experiences of the young mothers with those of a peer group who managed to avoid premature parenthood.

_____ , Richard Lincoln, and Jane Menken, Ed. *Teenage Sexuality, Pregnancy and Childbearing.* 1980. 423 pp. University of Pennsylvania Press, 3933 Walnut Street, Philadelphia, PA 19104. $10.50.

Over the past decade. Family Planning Perspectives has published much, if not most, of the research on the causes, consequences, and means of coping with problems associated with teenage pregnancy and childbearing. From about 100 articles, the editors selected 28 key reports for this book. Included is "Marriage, Remarriage, Marital Disruption and Age at First Birth" by James McCarthy and Jane Menken.

Galper, Miriam. *The Joint Custody and Co-Parenting Handbook.* 1980. $6.95. Running Press, 125 South 22nd Street, Philadelphia, PA 19103.

Galper describes in a very personal way co-parenting, the alternative to the more traditional forms of custody arrangements. In this system the child spends equal time with each parent, and each parent assumes an equal share of all child care responsibilities.

Garrett, Yvonne. *The Newlywed Handbook: A Refreshing, Practical Guide for Living Together.* 1981. $8.95. Word, Inc., 4800 Waco Drive, Waco, TX 76796.

The Newlywed Handbook is another easy-to-read and interesting book. The usual topics of intimacy, in-laws and family, communication, fighting, and money are covered. Also included are discussions of emotional and personality differences, managing time, having fun, enjoying friends, and family rituals. It's a short book, one that teenagers might enjoy.

Heinowitz, Jack. *Pregnant Fathers: How Fathers Can Enjoy and Share the Experiences of Pregnancy and Childbirth.* 1982. 126 pp. $5.95. Prentice-Hall, Inc., Rte. 9W, Englewood Cliffs, NJ 07632.

This is a book for the man who truly wants to be completely involved in "their" pregnancy. Primary focus is on feelings and changing relationships. Young couples eager to share the experience of pregnancy may find this book helpful.

Gribben, Trish. *Pajamas Don't Matter (or: What Your Baby Really Needs).* Illustrated by Dick Frizzell. 1980. Jalmar Press, Inc., 6501 Elvas Avenue, Sacramento, CA 95819. 50 pp. $5.95.

In 50 pages this book covers astonishingly well the really important aspects of parenting. Illustrations are colorful and funny.

Hansen, Caryl. *Your Choice: A Young Woman's Guide to Making Decisions About Unmarried Pregnancy.* 1980. Paper. $1.95. Avon Books, 959 Eighth Ave., New York, NY 10019.

This fills the need for a comprehensive, up-to-date book on the options open to pregnant teenagers. The author emphasizes the need for choosing an option rather than going into motherhood without making a decision. A chapter on the marriage option is included.

Head, Ann. *Mr. and Mrs. Bo Jo Jones.* 1973. 189 pp. $1.50. Signet Book. The American Library, Inc., 1633 Broadway, New York, NY 10019.

This story of a 16-year-old bride and 17-year-old groom who married because of pregnancy is an all-time favorite for teenagers.

Howard, Marion. *Only Human — Teenage Pregnancy and Parenthood.* 1979. Paper. Avon Books. 251 pp. $1.50.

An easily read story about three young couples expecting their first child. One couple is married. Interspersed throughout the story is a running commentary about the developmental aspects of both young women and young men as they go through the pregnancy and parenting experience.

Leman, Dr. Kevin. *Sex Begins in the Kitchen — Renewing Emotional and Physical Intimacy in Marriage.* $8.95. Regal Books, 2300 Knoll Drive, Ventura, CA 93003.

While Dr. Leman is not writing specifically to teenage couples, his book is a wonderful resource for couples of any age. It's interesting and easy to read, two necessary factors for attracting teenagers. His point that sex is an all-day affair, based on the couple's total relationship is an important concept. He uses lots of examples from his experience as a marriage and family counselor and in presenting Family Living Seminars throughout the country. His writing style is witty and funny. It's a delightful book.

Lewis, Howard R., and Martha E. *The Parents' Guide to Teenage Sex and Pregnancy.* 1980. 351 pp. Hardcover. St. Martin's Press, 175 Fifth Avenue, New York, NY 10010. $12.95.

Designed to help parents and professionals deal frankly and knowledgeably with the important sex-related issues affecting teenagers today. The last section deals with ways a parent can help a daughter or a son's girlfriend deal with early pregnancy. Marriage is discussed as one option.

Lindsay, Jeanne Warren. *Do I Have a Daddy? A Story About a Single-Parent Child.* Illustrated by DeeDee Upton Warr. 1982. 46 pp. Hardcover. Color. Morning Glory Press, 6595 San Haroldo Way, Buena Park, CA 90620. $7.95; 5/$35; 10/$65.

This is a picture book/story in which a single mother explains to her son that his daddy left soon after he was born. It contains a 12-page section of suggestions for single parents on how to deal with the question, "Do I have a daddy?"

_____ . *Pregnant Too Soon: Adoption Is an Option.* 1980. 208 pp. Morning Glory Press. Hardcover: $13.95. Paper: $6.95. Also published by EMC Publishing, St. Paul, Minnesota.

Young women who were, by their own admission, "pregnant too soon," speak for themselves. They share their reasons for making this tremendously difficult choice of releasing a baby for adoption. Several adult adoptees and adoptive parents also discuss their experiences. Included with the personal stories is the latest information on agency and independent adoption, fathers' rights, dealing with grief, and other aspects of adoption.

_____ . *Teens Parenting: The Challenge of Babies and Toddlers.* 1981. 308 pp. Illustrated by Pam Patterson Morford. Morning Glory Press. Hardcover: $14.95. Paper: $9.95. Teacher's Guide, 96 pp., paper, $5.95. Student Study Guide, 48 pp., stpld., $2.50.

The author interviewed 61 teenage mothers, then incorporated their comments and suggestions into each chapter. It focuses on "standard" child-rearing topics plus such special aspects of teenage parenthood as single parenting, father's involvement, costs of childrearing, three-generation living, need for education and job training for mothers, and help from community resources.

McCoy, Kathy, and Charles Wibbelsman, M.D. *The Teenage Body Book.* 1979. $5.95. A Wallaby Book published by Pocket Books, 1230 Avenue of the Americas, New York, NY 10020.

This is a book crammed with information for teenagers about everything from their bodies, changing feelings, teenage beauty, and special medical needs of young adults to sexuality, venereal disease, birth control, pregnancy and parenthood. The book is written directly to teenagers. Lots of quotes from young people, sometimes in the form of questions, are included in each chapter.

McGinnis, Dr. Tom. *Your First Year of Marriage.* 1977. Wilshire Book Company, 12015 Sherman Road, North Hollywood, CA 91605. $3.00.

While this is not a new book, it offers help in making the first year of marriage a good experience. Dr. McGinnis discusses such matters as adjustments husband and wife must make, the causes of disagreement and how they can be handled constructively, how to cope with in-laws, and other topics.

Miklowitz, Gloria. *The Day the Senior Class Got Married.* 1983. $12.95. Delacourte Press, c/o Dell Publishing Co., 1 Dag Hammarskjold Plaza, 245 E. 47th Street, New York, NY 10017.

This is a novel about a young couple, both seniors in high school, who are planning to be married. They take a high school economics class in which each student is paired with another in order to do research as a couple on the practical aspects of marriage.

As the months pass, Lori realizes she is a future-oriented person while her boyfriend lives for the present. The book provides a good and highly interesting description of some of the problems which can occur in such a situation.

Moore, Kristin A., Sandra L. Hofferth, Steven B. Caldwell, and Linda J. Waite. *Teenage Motherhood: Social and Economic Consequences.* 1979. $4.00. The Urban Institute, 2100 M Street, N.W., Washington, D.C. 20037.

This well-researched report focuses on the effects of early childbirth on the later social and economic status of the mother and her family. Education, family size, marriage and marital instability, participation in the labor force and earnings, welfare receipt, and poverty are analyzed separately. This 50-page book provides extremely important background information for anyone needing data to support special programs for pregnant minors, school-age parents, and for the prevention of early pregnancy.

Planned Parenthood Federation of America. *Teenage Pregnancy: The Problem That Hasn't Gone Away.* 1981. The Alan Guttmacher Institute, A Corporation for Research, Policy Analysis, and Public Education, 360 Park Avenue South, New York, NY 10010. 80 pp. $5.00. Bulk rates available.

Quite comprehensive and detailed, this booklet benefits from the considerable research undertaken in the 1970s. Purpose is "to assemble the facts in a way that will make reaching a reasoned solution more possible and less painful than it has been in the past." The final section, "Can the Problem Be Solved?" discusses the need for more adequate sex education for young people and increased availability of contraceptive information and devices.

Richards, Arlene K., and Irene Willis. *What To Do If You or Someone You Know Is Under 18 and Pregnant.* 256 pp. Paper. $7.00. Lothrop, Lee and Shepard Books, 105 Madison Avenue, New York, NY 10016.

The authors offer a good discussion of the alternatives available to pregnant adolescents.

Walker, Lenore. *The Battered Woman.* 1979. Paper, $4.95. Harper and Row Publishers, Inc., 10 E. 53rd Street, New York, NY.

At least half the women in the United States are hit by their husbands or boyfriends at some time, according to Ms. Walker. Her book contains many disturbing case studies. It also includes sections on preventive education, practical remedies including shelters, and a discussion of psychotherapy.

Weeks, John R. *Teenage Marriages — A Demographic Analysis.* 1976. $18.95. Greenwood Press, 88 Post Road West, P.O. Box 5007, Westport, CT 06881.

This is a detailed report of a study started in 1970 as part of a larger program of investigation into fertility and family formation at International Population and Urban Research (IPUR), University of California, Berkeley. It is a good discussion of teenage marriage in the United States. Included are lots of statistics through 1973.

Witt, Reni L., and Jeannine Masterson Michael. *Mom, I'm Pregnant — A Personal Guide for Teenagers.* 1982. 239 pp. $6.95. Stein & Day, Scarborough House, Briarcliff Manor, NY 10510.

This is an excellent book for young women who are pregnant or think they may be — a guide to help them make important decisions. It is written in a personal, clear, easy-to-read and non-judgmental manner. Essential information about marriage, keeping the baby, adoption, foster care, and abortion is included. It realistically explains the pros and cons of each choice and how it might affect the teenager and the important people in her life.

ABOUT THE AUTHOR

Jeanne Warren Lindsay has worked closely with hundreds of teenagers during the past eleven years. She is resource specialist/teacher for the ABC Unified School District Teen Mother Program at Tracy High School, Cerritos, California. Most pregnant students in the district, married and single, choose to attend this program rather than continue at their regular schools during pregnancy. After delivery, many young mothers enroll their babies in the Tracy Infant Center, then continue their own education at the school where Ms. Lindsay teaches a daily parenting class.

Jeanne and Bob Lindsay have been married for almost a third of a century. Their five grown children are scattered across the United States.

Ms. Lindsay has an M.A. in Anthropology and an M.A. in Home Economics from California State University, Long Beach. She is a member of the Board of Directors of the National Organization on Adolescent Pregnancy and Parenthood and of the California Alliance Concerned with School-Age Parents.

Previous books by Ms. Lindsay include *Pregnant Too Soon: Adoption Is An Option, Teens Parenting: The Challenge of Babies and Toddlers,* and *Do I Have a Daddy? A Story About a Single-Parent Child.*

Index

AFDC (Aid to Families with Dependent Children), 47, 98
Anger, 63-68, 182
Arguments, 46, 63-68, 182
Attitude survey, 14-15, 24, 29, 33, 34-35, 42, 52, 58, 59-60, 72-73, 86, 87, 95, 114, 131, 133, 142-143, 190-196

Barr, Linda, 129
Battered Woman, The, 157, 159
Bayard, Bob, Ph.D., and Jean, Ph.D., 65, 91, 93
Blau, Rita, 44-45, 170
Brainstorming, 65
Brunelli, Jean, 78-79
Budget, 102, 104-111

Career planning, 43, 47, 100-101
Changes in marriage, 50-55
Charge cards, 110
Child abuse, 156-157
Child custody, 172, 173-174
Childbirth, effect on sexuality, 77-80
Childcare, 127-139; Sharing, 40, 80, 93; classes, 135-136
Chores, 53, 114-115, 118-127, 167
Closson, Dr. Charles, 24, 38
Communication, 32, 46, 58-69, 72, 75
Compromise, 73
Co-parenting, 174
Counseling, 161, 163, 168, 170-172
Crisis Center, 156, 163

Day the Senior Class Got Married, The, 40
Diapers, cost of, 137-138
Divorce, 11, 13, 21, 149, 166-170, 172-174, 185; Grief after, 172

Education, importance of, 13, 26-27, 28, 47, 130
Equal marriage, 84-95
Ethnicity, 45, 122
Expense record, 105-106
Extended family, 14, 39, 85, 114-125, 169, 179

Falling in love, 24-25

Family planning, 78, 138-139
Feedback in communication, 65
Freedom, loss of, 52
Freemon, Van, 155-157, 158, 160
Friends, effect of marriage on, 52, 146-148; moving in with, 124
Future/Present orientation, 40, 111

Galper, Miriam, 174
Grandparents, 136
Greenbaum, Marvin, 61
Gribben, Trish, 79
Gunny-sacking, 68
Housework, 53-54, 119-121, 122, 167
How to Deal with Your Acting-Up Teenager, 65

I-messages, 64
Immaturity, 167
In-laws, 14, 45, 54, 69, 85, 114-125
Infidelity, 76, 149-150

Jealousy, 44, 47, 131-132, 141-151
Joint Custody and Co-Parenting Handbook, 174

Law, teenage marriage, 24
Legal help, 172
Leman, Dr. Kevin, 72, 81
Living together, 33-34
Loneliness in marriage, 54

Marriage Is for Grown-Ups, 168
Marriage scorecard, 47, 188-189
Marriage statistics, 13, 14, 24, 166
McCoy, Kathy, 72
McGinnis, Dr. Tom, 39, 41
Miklowitz, Gloria, 40
Money, 46, 47, 65, 84, 86, 88, 98-111, 114, 121, 136-138
Monserrat, Catherine, 11-12, 129
Music, 44

Pajamas Don't Matter, 79
Parental support, 47, 52, 88
Parenthood, 51, 127-139; classes, 135-136, 175; decision, 40, 138-139
Peach, Ellen, 74

Ping-pong method of
  communication, 65
Possessiveness, 146-148
Pregnancy, 14, 25, 27-31, 32, 51, 73,
  114, 123, 128-129, 144, 178, 180,
  184-185
Prepared childbirth, 129, 134
Present/Future orientation, 40, 111
Privacy, 55, 73, 116-118

Rape, 155
Religion, 45-46
Remarriage, 174-175
Role-sharing, 40, 41, 53, 84-95

San Francisco Family Violence
  Project, 158
Scripts, family, 69, 167-168
Self-esteem, 47, 144-145, 167
Separation, 179

Sex, 61, 72-81
Sex Begins in the Kitchen, 72, 81
Six-months rule, 149
Step-children, 175

Teenage Body Book, 72
*Teenage Pregnancy: A New
  Beginning*, 129
*Teens Parenting: The Challenge of
  Babies and Toddlers*, 128, 157
Traditional marriage, 40, 84-85, 88-91
Trust, 143, 146, 147, 149, 151, 183

Walker, Lenore E., 157, 159
Wibbelsman, Charles, 72
Wife-battering, 47, 143, 153-163; effect
  on children, 160-161
Wish list, 68

Your First Year of Marriage, 39

PHOTO CREDITS

David Crawford........Pages 61, 75, 82, 92, 94, 96, 107, 126, 176, 181
Vicki Strauss Golini.........Pages 31, 41, 48, 56, 70, 80, 117, 133, 164
Bob Lindsay.............Pages 36, 66, 90, 112, 121, 137, 140, 147, 205
Joyce Young, Buchner & Young Photography................Page 19
Dave Hefner, Animated Art.........................Cover Design

MAIL ORDER FORM

Teenage Marriage: Coping with Reality

Trade: $8.95; Cloth: $14.95
48-page Consumable Study Guide: $2.50
(Quantity Discount Available)

Other Books by Jeanne Lindsay

Teens Parenting: The Challenge of Babies and Toddlers
A parenting book written especially for very young parents. Includes many comments and suggestions from young mothers. Excellent for Child Development/Parenting classes.
Trade: $9.95; Cloth: $14.95
Teacher's Guide: $5.95; Student Study Guide: $2.50
(Quantity Discounts on Book and Study Guides)

Pregnant Too Soon: Adoption Is an Option
Latest information on adoption together with personal stories of young birth mothers who released their babies for adoption.
Trade: $6.95; Cloth: $13.95
Consumable Student Study Guide, 16 pages: $1.00; 10/$5.00
(Quantity Discount on Cloth Edition Only)

Do I Have a Daddy? A Story About a Single-Parent Child
Picture story for children whose parents never married.
Includes 10-page section of suggestions for single parents.
Cloth: $7.95
(Quantity Discount)

- -

MORNING GLORY PRESS
6595-B San Haroldo Way
Buena Park, CA 90620

Quantity		Price	Total
	Teenage Marriage: Coping with Reality		
_____	Trade, ISBN 0-930934-11-3	$8.95	_____
_____	Cloth, ISBN 0-930934-12-1	$14.95	_____
_____	Consumable Study Guide	$2.50	_____
	Teens Parenting: The Challenge of Babies and Toddlers		
_____	Trade, ISBN 0-930934-06-7	$9.95	_____
_____	Cloth, ISBN 0-930934-07-5	$14.95	_____
_____	Teacher's Guide, ISBN 0-930934-09-1	$5.95	_____
_____	Student Study Guide, ISBN 0-930934-08-3 . . . . . $2.50, 10/$20.00		_____
	Pregnant Too Soon: Adoption Is an Option		
_____	Trade, ISBN 0-88436-778-9	$6.95	_____
_____	Cloth, ISBN 0-930934-05-9	$13.95	_____
	Do I Have a Daddy?		
_____	Cloth, ISBN 0-930934-10-5	$7.95	_____
		TOTAL	_____

Please add 10% postage/handling (min. $1.50, max. $10.00) _____
California residents add 6% sales tax _____
TOTAL ENCLOSED _____

NAME _____

ADDRESS_____

_____